# THE TRANSATLANTIC
# DRIFT DEBATES

# THE TRANSATLANTIC DRIFT DEBATES

## Proceedings from the American Foreign Policy Council's 2004 Conference on U.S.-European Relations

LEXINGTON BOOKS

A division of
ROWMAN & LITTLEFIELD PUBLISHERS, INC.
Lanham • Boulder • New York • Toronto • Plymouth, UK

LEXINGTON BOOKS

A division of Rowman & Littlefield Publishers, Inc.
A wholly owned subsidiary of The Rowman & Littlefield Publishing Group, Inc.
4501 Forbes Boulevard, Suite 200
Lanham, MD 20706

Estover Road
Plymouth PL6 7PY
United Kingdom

British Library Cataloguing in Publication Information Available

**Library of Congress Cataloging-in-Publication Data**

The transatlantic drift debates : proceedings from the American Foreign Policy Council's
2004 conference on U.S.-European relations.
    p. cm.
  Conference sponsored by the American Foreign Policy Council and the Prague Society.
  ISBN-13: 978-0-7391-1661-6 (cloth : alk. paper)
  ISBN-10: 0-7391-1661-4 (cloth : alk. paper)
  ISBN-13: 978-0-7391-1662-3 (pbk. : alk. paper)
  ISBN-10: 0-7391-1662-2 (pbk. : alk. paper)
  1. Europe—Relations—United States—Congresses. 2. United States—Relations—
Europe—Congresses. I. American Foreign Policy Council. II. Prague Society for
International Cooperation.

  D2025.5.U64T73 2006
  327.7304—dc22                                                          2006024848

Printed in the United States of America

∞™ The paper used in this publication meets the minimum requirements of American
National Standard for Information Sciences—Permanence of Paper for Printed Library
Materials, ANSI/NISO Z39.48-1992.

# Contents

Preface     vii

    Ilan Berman

**Introductory Remarks**

    Herman Pirchner Jr.     3
    Rt. Hon. Lord Malcolm Pearson of Rannoch     7

**Panel I: Can Political/Military Tensions Lead to a Disruption of Economic Relations between the U.S. and Europe?**

    The Hon. Jim Saxton     13
    Amb. Stuart E. Eizenstat     17
    The Hon. Jans Held Madsen     25
    The Hon. Barbara McDougall     27
    Dr. Richard Rahn     29

**Panel II: Under What Conditions Is a Transatlantic Political Consensus on the Use of Force Possible?**

    The Hon. Curt Weldon     35
    The Hon. Lothar Binding     39
    Dr. John Lenczowski     43

**Panel III: What Role Has the Media Played in U.S.-European Relations?**

| | |
|---|---:|
| Martin Walker | 47 |
| Georg Schmolz | 55 |
| John Fund | 59 |
| John O'Sullivan | 63 |
| Roland Flamini | 69 |

**Panel IV: Do Objective Differences in National Interests Dictate a Fundamental Shift in the U.S.-Europe Relationship?**

| | |
|---|---:|
| The Hon. Mark Lagon | 75 |
| The Hon. Dov Zakheim | 79 |
| Yossef Bodansky | 81 |
| Carl Gershman | 85 |

# Preface

## Ilan Berman

### Vice President for Policy, American Foreign Policy Council

I T IS NO SECRET that diplomatic relations between the United States and Europe have seen better days. The transatlantic unity that punctuated the early days of the Global War on Terror has sadly dissipated, and Washington and European capitals now find themselves on opposing sides of a grave—and growing—strategic rift. A range of issues, including war in Iraq, America's perceived foreign policy unilateralism, and the future direction of the struggle against the scourge of international terrorism, have emerged to challenge the durability of America's longest-running diplomatic, economic, and strategic alliance.

A desire to bridge this growing divide lies at the heart of the "TransAtlantic Drift Debates," a series of high-level meetings begun in 2003 with the goal of bringing together top American and European statesmen, policymakers, and officials in government. In the summer of 2004, the American Foreign Policy Council had the privilege of hosting the fourth installment of this prestigious discussion in Washington, D.C. The pages that follow contain the presentations of the majority of the conference participants. They have been edited for style and tone, but not for substance.

It is our sincere hope that through them, the United States and Europe begin to find the common ground to restore the vitality of their historic relationship, and to build a foundation for a true twenty-first-century partnership.

# Introductory Remarks

# Herman Pirchner Jr.

## President, American Foreign Policy Council

TODAY'S GATHERING IS THE FOURTH in a series of conferences on the so-called TransAtlantic Drift—the political differences now affecting ties between the U.S. and Europe. The American Foreign Policy Council is pleased to join the Prague Society in cohosting these discussions as one of the many steps that need to be taken—in the interests of both Europe and the United States—to bring our respective foreign and defense policies into greater harmony.

Some context, however, is necessary. American-European relations, while not good, are not as bad as they have been in the past. Since the founding of the United States, Americans have fought wars with all of the major European states (although the one with the former USSR was a cold one). In the last sixty years alone, American blood has been spilled by the forces of Nazi Germany, Fascist Italy, and Vichy France. Today, fortunately, no one seriously thinks that war between the U.S. and any country in Europe is possible. Since the Cold War's end, American relations with Eastern European countries have improved dramatically. However, our friendly relations with Western European countries have cooled considerably. The question is why.

The paramount reason is the lack of a universally recognized common enemy. Even at the time when 25 percent of the French and Italian electorates were voting along communist lines, the governments of those and other Western European countries, as well as the majority of their populations, stood with the U.S. in its fight against Soviet Communism. Today, however, the USSR is gone, and most in Western Europe do not see a serious threat to their well-being. And if there is no threat, the argument goes, then there is no need for Western Europe to follow the militarily superior

United States. Nor is there any need to create serious European defense forces within Western Europe.

Some in Europe go even further, believing that if there is no threat, any military action taken by the U.S. may do more harm than good by stirring up threats like the one now posed by radical Islam. To their thinking, American behavior in the world must therefore be restrained by international organizations where Europeans play a leading role. In explaining this position, Henry Kissinger noted that: "Because the historic rivalries of Europe have been civilized into a domestic consensus, European diplomats seek to apply their new domestic experience in the international arena."

To the extent that Kissinger's formulation is true, most Americans would view these European diplomats as departed from reality. Those who perpetrated the recent genocide and forced dislocations in Africa, or the leadership of al-Qaeda, are not likely to settle their differences with the West through reasoned argument and devotion to the norms of international law. Most Americans believe a common threat to Western societies exists, and will continue to exist in the foreseeable future. In the words of former U.S. secretary of state Alexander Haig:

> Our cities were attacked but others have also been attacked in Europe, the Middle East, Africa, and Asia. It is a global struggle with global stakes for the international order. . . . If we allow terrorism to become the method of advancement in international relations, then all progress will be jeopardized—freedom, security, and prosperity lost.

Following the terror attacks in Madrid, there are some signs that Europe is beginning to take this threat more seriously, but divisions with the U.S. remain. This is true for two major reasons: First, Western European countries are reluctant to use their limited military capability, and second, they have no serious plans to increase that capability.

For a minute, let us focus on Germany and France. When France was in agreement on the post–9/11 campaign in Afghanistan, it managed to send only 800 troops to Afghanistan in support of America's efforts. Germany sent 2,300 troops—its largest foreign troop deployment since World War II. And what of the capability of those troops—troops that are certainly welcome and needed? They are able to provide a supporting function, but have limited capability to operate on their own. They are underequipped and technologically deficient. In short, one can argue that the military value of their participation is less than the value of their diplomacy and foreign aid.

Additionally, the cost of political and military assistance from Germany and France is increasingly considered too high. Leading up to the Iraq War, the Bush administration viewed France and Germany's prescriptions as unworkable at worst, and at best as demanding compromises that were not worth the support given in return. This view hearkened back to our experience in the Balkans, where Europe's failure to manage the disintegration of Yugoslavia led to a U.S. military involvement that was bedeviled by European political interference.

This is not to say that European diplomatic support and foreign aid are worthless. On the contrary, they have great value. UN support still carries legitimacy in the world and Europe's combined foreign aid budget is bigger than that of the U.S. The question is, therefore, one of price—and it is not a new question for anyone in international politics.

When the Allied invasion of North Africa began in 1942, much of the territory in question was held by French troops whose leadership was loyal to the Fascist government in Vichy. This led the Allies to search for alternative leadership. The ideal candidate seemed to be the recently retired anti-Fascist General Henri Giraud, whose stature, it was thought, might rally the French troops to at least neutrality. After tentative acceptance of this idea, Giraud was secretly brought to Gibraltar to meet General Eisenhower. There, without a single French soldier to fight with him on the Allied side, he demanded to be named supreme allied commander in the French North as soon as Allied forces landed in French territory. After Eisenhower enumerated all the reasons why this was not possible, Giraud announced that he could not take a lesser role because to do so would be to tarnish his honor as a soldier. Instead, he would merely be a spectator in the war. Yet after a period of reflection, an accommodation was finally reached and General Giraud agreed to command the French forces that had accepted a ceasefire, following the loss of over 1,000 American lives in combat with the troops of Vichy France.

It is the hope of the American Foreign Policy Council, and I believe of the Prague Society as well, that today's discussions will cause all of us to reflect on both the advantages of cooperation and the disadvantages of noncooperation. I believe the case for increased European-American cooperation to be very strong. But, if national interests, as they are perceived today, militate against closer cooperation in the near future, let these discussions serve as part of the basis for closer ties when the political environment either permits or dictates it.

I have no doubt that that time will come.

# The Right Honorable
# Lord Malcolm Pearson of Rannoch

## Member, House of Lords of Great Britain

IT IS A GREAT, IF SOMEWHAT SURPRISING, honor to be asked to join in welcoming such a distinguished audience. It is surprising because I have been invited to this conference as the obligatory but sole Euro-skeptic from perfidious Albion—or little old Britain, if you prefer.

My only qualification for this honor is that I do speak for the growing millions of British people, already perhaps around half the population, who want the United Kingdom to leave the European Union as soon as possible. This is because they are starting to see that in 1975, the only time they have ever been asked, they were deceived into voting to stay in what they were assured was a free trade area. They now see that the EU has turned out to be a very different animal; one which has already stealthily devoured much of their democracy—for which so many of them, and so many of you, have died over the centuries.

Ladies and Gentlemen, here at least is one European, speaking again on behalf of the Euro-skeptic millions back home, who would like to place on record his unqualified and most heartfelt thanks to *you*, the United States of America, for the colossal sacrifices you have made for us in two World Wars; and more, much more.

The *idea* behind the EU Project was perhaps honorable and understandable in its day, even if it has turned out to be very misguided. This idea was that nation-states had been responsible for the carnage of two World Wars, and, therefore, the nation-states—national democracies—must be emasculated and diluted into a new form of supranational government, run by a Commission of wise technocrats. That, in its barest form, is still the EU Project.

It is worth emphasizing that the word "Europe" has come to have two sharply contrasting meanings. One is the Europe of different democracies, which we all know and love, each with its glorious history and culture. The other has come to be the Project of the EU, based in Brussels on the Treaties of Rome. I speak to you as a good European in the former meaning of the word. We Euro-skeptics love the Europe of Nations. What we fear and dislike intensely is the corrupt octopus in Brussels, and all of its works.

How does this Project come to destroy democracy? I submit that the heart of any genuine democracy is the right of the people to elect and dismiss those who make their laws. You may not be aware how the EU's system of lawmaking bypasses national parliaments, elected by the people, and turns them into rubber stamps. Very briefly, the EU's appointed bureaucracy, the Commission, enjoys the monopoly to propose new laws in secret. The Council of Ministers from national governments then adopts those laws, again by secret vote, and—if the national parliaments don't enact them—their countries face unlimited fines in the Luxembourg "court."

In huge areas of our national life, our executive can be outvoted in the Council of Ministers, where the United Kingdom has 11 percent of the 30 percent needed to block a new law. For the record, those areas are: all of our commerce and industry; our social and labor policy; our agriculture, fish, environment, foreign aid, and foreign trade relations. Furthermore, Parliament must also rubber-stamp all new laws *agreed* to by the Executive in the areas of foreign and security policy, and even justice and home affairs, or we would be in breach of our treaty obligations. The Executive can refuse to agree to new legislation in these areas, but if it does not, Parliament and the people are stuck with them. No law made in Brussels has ever been overturned by a national parliament.

That is how bad it is now, but worse is on the way. National governments have just signed on to a new Constitution, which finally removes any pretence that the EU is a treaty-based arrangement between consenting democracies. The EU is to be given its own legal personality, superior to that of the nation-states, and nearly all the remaining areas of our national life, which used to be under the control of the House of Commons, will become subject to majority voting in Brussels. Even the veto power of national governments disappears almost entirely.

This new Constitution will be subject to referenda in most EU states, and we in Britain have a good chance of throwing it out. It is difficult to predict what will happen if we do, because the Constitution has to be ratified by all twenty-five participant nations. Technically, we all stay where we are, which is already unacceptable.

But this EU Project also holds great dangers for the United States, and for American democracy. First, of course, the Project imperils the Atlantic Alliance, as we have seen over Iraq. Indeed, the Project's main raison d'être, driven by France's deep, psychotic need to bite the hand that freed her in two World Wars, has become to build a bloc powerful enough to undermine the United States and NATO. They are quite open about this in Brussels.

Then, as the EU economy continues its downward trend, thanks to Europe's declining demographics and to the Franco-German social and labor policies which the Project forces on all its members, the second danger is that the U.S. business community will find its investments in Europe increasingly disappointing.

Third, and perhaps most frightening of all, the U.S. Supreme Court is already starting to take note of the politically correct judgments from the European Courts in Luxembourg, Strasbourg, and the Hague. This trend will increase, and seriously weaken America's own democracy.

I honestly believe it is in America's interest to take a closer look at this EU Project. Once it does, I trust it will find that its interests lie in working with those of us who wish to see democracy in Europe restored to where it belongs: to the great democracies of Europe, to the nation-states, freely trading together, linked through NATO, and going forward in harmony with the United States of America, whom may God bless.

# I

# Can Political/Military Tensions Lead to a Disruption of Economic Relations between the U.S. and Europe?

# The Honorable Jim Saxton

## Member, United States House of Representatives (R-NJ)

I APPROACH THIS SUBJECT from what is perhaps an interesting perspective. First, I have had the opportunity and the honor to serve as the Chairman of the Joint Economic Committee, which is often referred to as the "think tank" of Congress. Second, for the past two years I have had the unique opportunity to serve as the Chairman of the Subcommittee on Terrorism of the House Armed Services Committee.

There are several reasons why I expect the economic relationship between the U.S. and Europe to remain very important, despite some recent disagreements on military and related political issues. This is not to say that there will not be disputes from time to time. But serious disruption in our economic relationship is, in my view, improbable. That is because there are several cornerstones of the transatlantic relationship which are as important today as they were before the disagreement over Iraq.

The transatlantic alliance served as a beacon of freedom through the dark years of the Cold War. Our shared beliefs in freedom, democracy, and the rule of law are more than capable of bridging our differences in the face of common threats. Together, the United States and the European Union believe wholeheartedly in eradicating terrorism and are working together to destroy illicit black market trading, especially in the areas of weapons of mass destruction and narcotics.

Along with our European friends, we share a deep commitment to the rules and norms of international and free market capitalism. Economic relations between America and Europe are long-standing and deeply rooted in historic ties, going back to a time when European countries established colonies in

North America. These economic ties have survived a number of policy disagreements, and are unlikely to be disrupted by recent discord over policy matters because of underlying economic realities.

In terms of goods and services, the Europeans are our largest trading partners, and the reverse is true as well. Extensive trade exists because it is very much in the interest of both Europe and the U.S. Moreover, American firms are the largest investors in Europe and European firms are the largest foreign investors in the U.S. The EU is not a unified state but an entity of twenty-five separate nations, each of which seems to have retained substantial autonomy over many years.

The diversity of interests within Europe makes it less likely to emerge soon as a unified block fundamentally hostile to American interests, despite the efforts of some. As a result, the Europeans will be our trading partners and competitors in a continuing economic relationship for the foreseeable future, eclipsing disagreements in other areas. After all, history has shown that the U.S. has expanded economic relations with countries that are more potentially problematic than those in Europe, irrespective of whether or not this was a wise thing to do.

Recently, obvious differences in policy regarding Iraq have become a major source of tension between the U.S. and several European countries. Two of the major countries that founded the EU, France and Germany, have been the most problematic and uncooperative regarding the Coalition effort to depose Saddam Hussein and facilitate the development of democracy in Iraq. Whether motivated by misguided balance of power notions, jealousy, anti-Americanism, or even anti-Semitism, European opposition to Coalition actions in Europe has damaged our political relations with France and Germany.

These countries were not content merely to register their opposition to the Coalitions' actions, but actively sought to undermine and obstruct them. This active hostility has led to American frustration and some boycotting of goods, especially in reaction to the particularly obstructive actions of the French government.

As one American wag expressed the popular American reaction, "50 million Frenchmen can be wrong." However, it is also essential to emphasize that Europe did not act in unison with regard to Iraq. The United Kingdom was a leading member of the Coalition from the beginning, and several other European countries, such as Poland and Italy, have also been supportive.

In the weeks leading up to the onset of Operation Iraqi Freedom, I was deeply concerned by the attempts of some of our European allies to publicly humiliate the United States. However, the fundamental cornerstones of the transatlantic relationship remain intact, and are needed in order for us to be victorious in the War on Terror. At the heart of these ties is our mutually prosperous economic relationship, which I believe will continue into the future.

The economic ties between America and Europe go back to the Colonial Era. From the start, American economic development was highly dependent upon the importation of both capital and labor from Europe. Indeed, America relied heavily on European capital throughout its industrialization into the early part of the last century. At present, hundreds of billions of dollars of goods and services are exchanged each year between America and Europe. Bilateral direct investment is yet another indicator of our diverse economic relationship. U.S. direct investment and European facilities owned by U.S. individuals and corporations amounted to $845 billion in 2003.

At the same time, the EU has invested about $856 billion in facilities located in the U.S. This two-way flow of investment is the most substantial in the world. As a result, nearly four million European workers have jobs created by U.S. investment, and a similar number of Americans have jobs tied to European investment. The economic ties reflected in those trade and investment figures highlight extensive mutual economic interest.

Since this trade and investment relationship is in the economic interest of both America and Europe, it is difficult to see noneconomic factors becoming a serious and long-lasting disruptive force. The economic self-interest of both the U.S. and Europe make the relationship mutually beneficial and financially compelling. It is my hope that the tensions revolving around differing views of Iraq will begin to recede, and that all European countries will be able to play a constructive role in the creation of a new government in Iraq.

# The Honorable Stuart E. Eizenstat

Former Deputy Secretary of Treasury,
United States; Former United States
Ambassador to the European Union

THE U.S.-LED WAR AGAINST IRAQ has exposed both the most fundamental difference between the United States and Europe since the U.S.-supported creation of the European Coal and Steel Community to heal European divisions after World War II, as well as highlighting the deep fissures within Europe itself regarding the transatlantic relationship.

We used to define a crisis in European-U.S. relations as trade disputes over beef and bananas. We could only wish for such crises today. We are currently seeing the most profound gulf in our relationship since the end of World War II. In mid-October, a Euro Barometer poll of European public opinion showed that 55 percent of respondents believed the U.S. to be the greatest threat to world peace, second only to Israel and higher than Iran, North Korea, Europe, Russia, and China. Something fundamental has gone wrong.

From the earliest days following World War II, the U.S. played a leadership role in helping to heal the European divisions that spawned two World Wars in the twentieth century. The Marshall Plan encouraged cooperation among former European enemies in planning their postwar reconstruction. For sixty years, the U.S. was a champion of greater European political and economic integration, and an unequivocal supporter of the EU's expansion and NATO's enlargement to the east, creating, for the first time in history, an undivided Europe organized around democratic, free market principles. For its part, Europe looked to a U.S.-led NATO for a robust defense against the common Soviet threat.

Two events caused our current crisis. One was November 9th, 1989—the day that the Berlin Wall fell and the Cold War effectively ended. The other was

September 11th, the terrorist attacks on the World Trade Center and the Pentagon. The first gave Europe a reason to disengage from the U.S. The second led the U.S. under the Bush administration to act independently of NATO and many of its European allies. By tying Iraq to the same terrorist threat that provoked 9/11, the U.S. and Europe now faced a war without a shared sense of danger.

Certainly, part of the problem is inevitable. The glue that held Europe and the U.S. together naturally eroded after the end of the Cold War. Some of the factors causing today's difficulties were simply submerged when there was a common threat. First, as the structures of its social and economic systems indicate, Europe occupies a major step to the left in the political spectrum. A traditional Christian Democrat in Europe would be akin to a moderate Democrat in the U.S. Second, having gone through the ravages of World War II, many in Europe have a reluctance to use force to resolve conflicts even when force is necessary, as in the Balkans. Third, Europe's large Muslim population and European attitudes toward Israel give Europe a different perspective on the Middle East than the U.S.

Iraq has exposed all of these fault lines, and has highlighted significant differences in the way Europe and the U.S. perceive threats to national security—from terrorism and weapons of mass destruction to global warming and Islamic fundamentalism; the approach to "rogue nations" that act outside of accepted international norms; the use of military force; the role of multinational institutions in settling international disagreements; and the limits of the EU's own "common foreign and security policy."

The EU believes that the best way to deal with difficult nations, from Cuba and Iran to Iraq, Syria, and North Korea, is through normal political and economic relations, transmitting Western norms. The U.S., particularly the U.S. Congress, instead has opted for isolation, sanctions, and even military force.

Likewise, the EU places much greater confidence in multilateral agreements and multilateral institutions like the United Nations than the Bush administration. George W. Bush ran for president criticizing the Clinton administration's penchant for multilateral consensus, and has followed through by abandoning international agreements from the Kyoto Treaty to the International Criminal Court. The Administration's reluctant use of, and ultimate dissatisfaction with, the United Nations inspection process in Iraq underscored the point.

The EU is, by its very nature, an institution in which sovereignty is shared. It needs the UN and other international bodies to maximize its influence in the world. By contrast, the Bush administration sees the UN as minimizing American influence and compromising America's sovereign interests.

Added to this is the fact that the EU has no ability to project military power; its members have a deep aversion to the use of military force under almost any circumstance, and have slashed their military budgets since the end of the Cold War. Merely the increase in the Pentagon's budget from this to the next fiscal year will be greater than the total military budget of any continental European nation. The ability of the U.S. to project its military might on a global scale leaves it with military options unavailable to Europe.

As if these differences were not profound enough, there is another: the Bush administration's daring doctrine of preemptive action against nations that may threaten America's interests but have not begun a conflict, one which resonates with a nation traumatized by September 11th and the threat of further terrorist actions against the United States.

The division in Europe over support for the U.S. in Iraq has also torn to shreds the EU's emerging common foreign policy. The crisis in EU-U.S. relations is mirrored in the internal crisis—between the UK, Spain, Portugal, Italy, and Poland on one side and France, Germany, and Belgium on the other—over Europe's future relationship with the United States in a post–Cold War world.

So what can now be done to restore some semblance of transatlantic cooperation, which is so important to the solution of world problems from the Israeli-Palestinian conflict to North Korea?

It is time for a new Atlantic Charter to chart our course for the twenty-first century and to provide a shared sense of direction. This should replace the new Transatlantic Agenda I helped to negotiate in 1995, which still forms the basis of the EU-U.S. relationship. It has been eclipsed by the dramatic developments in recent years, from September 11th to the EU enlargement to the Iraq war.

First, the Charter needs a new economic goal that takes into account the increased integration of our economies into a barrier-free transatlantic marketplace within ten years. All barriers to investment (e.g., airlines, communications) should be lifted; an integrated capital market created with mutually recognized accounting/audit standards and stock exchange listing requirements; and all products mutually accepted with only one set of tests in one market satisfying both markets (i.e., we would recognize the equivalence of each other's health, safety, and environmental regulations). Through the WTO, we should work toward the goal of zero tariffs on industrial goods. We should recognize each other's professional credentials and allow a free flow of professional workers.

It is imperative not to allow profound political differences to seep into our economic and trade relationship. The European and American economies are highly integrated and mutually dependent. At $2.5 trillion, we have the largest economic relationship in the world. U.S. and EU affiliates employ three million of each other's citizens in the U.S. and Europe. In tiny Ireland, with six million people, there is two times more U.S. investment than in China. Improved economic relations can provide the glue to hold our relationship together until a time when we restore our political relationships. Working together to launch the WTO Doha Round by July is another constructive EU-U.S. venture that reminds us of our shared economic interests. But we should go further.

The new Atlantic Charter should pledge a mutual focus on giving priority to multilateral trade liberalization. When we do bilateral FTAs, they should truly be consistent with WTO requirements and not be trade diverting or exclude major sectors like agriculture. The economic chapter of the new Atlantic Charter should also pledge to work cooperatively to deal with developing country challenges from HIV/AIDS to debt relief and democracy promotion.

Second, while leaving room for any country to act independently when it feels its national security requires it, the new Atlantic Charter should define in broad terms the ways we will deal with external threats. There should be a hierarchy of actions, in which we should pledge to make best efforts to act in a united fashion. We should first try to resolve crises by diplomacy, as we are doing in North Korea today. Diplomacy alone will often be insufficient. We should then seek multilateral, rather than unilateral, economic, political, and diplomatic sanctions. These have been effective from Apartheid-era South Africa to Serbia. Inspection regimes for WMD under the IAEA, having taken place under Hans Blix in Iraq and currently taking place in Iran, are part of this. But they can only work if Europe and America are committed to making them work, with tough sanctions in store for those who ignore them. When Saddam Hussein expelled the arms inspectors in the 1990s, firmer action should have been taken. Iran today will be a test case for firmness.

Military actions should be an option when others have failed. In cases which do not directly affect the national security interests of the U.S. and Europe but present grave humanitarian disasters, like Rwanda in 1994 and Sudan today, our Charter should pledge members to promptly seek UN Security Council support for UN peacekeeping action.

In cases where our security interests are directly threatened, there should be early and frequent dialogue to share intelligence and risk assessments. Many difficulties with Iraq might have been avoided had this been done. Whenever possible, UN approval should be sought. Gulf War I under President George H. Bush offers a model.

We should use NATO with UN support whenever possible. The NATO alliance must be the cornerstone of U.S. military efforts abroad, with its military assets, integrated military command and record of success in Europe and beyond. These are a precious resource. It is the best "force multiplier" the U.S. has. It must be the center of our international security policy, from dealing with the threat of terrorism to the prevention of the spread of WMD. To be relevant, NATO must act outside of Europe, as well as inside, when transatlantic interests are threatened. Even when NATO action is inappropriate, as in Haiti, for example, presents a case where French and U.S. military cooperation was welcome.

The new Atlantic Charter should also clearly define how the EU's emerging military capability, the Euro Corps, will be integrated into NATO.

One test of an improved relationship is helping govern and reconstruct a post-Saddam Iraq. With the new UN resolution, and the activities of the secretary general's special envoy to name an interim government in Iraq, there is a belated but welcome recognition by the Bush administration that there are limits to American unilateralism. We can win a war alone, but we cannot win the peace. Whatever one believes about the wisdom of going to war in Iraq, premature withdrawal is unthinkable—it would leave Iraq in chaos and further damage U.S. credibility. NATO has a role to play in training the Iraqi military and taking over some of the peacekeeping burden from the U.S. The reluctance of key NATO countries to do so reflects the reality that trying to bring in NATO after the fact, rather than at the outset of conflict, is the worst way to deal with our most important military alliance.

This is not the first misfire by the Administration regarding NATO. After 9/11, NATO invoked the Article 5 Mutual Defense provision for the first time in its history. There was unanimous desire to make the Afghanistan war against the Taliban and al-Qaeda a united NATO venture. Instead, the Administration ignored NATO and went into Afghanistan by itself, unilaterally. It is encouraging that NATO agreed to command the International Security Assistance Force that will soon grow to a 10,000-strong peacekeeping force. Yet, the lack of defense capability in Europe is demonstrated by the difficulty of delivering the modest number of helicopters and transport aircraft needed to extend the NATO presence beyond Kabul.

Likewise, at the June 2004 EU-U.S. Summit in Ireland and at the G8 Sea Island Summit, the president pleaded for economic assistance and debt relief in rebuilding Iraq—but to little effect. As difficult as it is, Europe needs to put aside its objections to the war, and work with the U.S. to build the peace. The future of Iraq is too important to permit peevishness to be a policy.

Third, the new Atlantic Charter should take advantage of a natural division of responsibilities in dealing with crises, with America's overwhelming military and diplomatic power, and the EU's substantial foreign assistance and nation-building capacity. The EU, together with its member states, has the largest foreign assistance budget in the world. The U.S. can take the military lead in NATO and assume a greater military burden, while the EU takes the lead in post-conflict peacekeeping and nation-building. That is precisely what is happening today in Bosnia and Kosovo. The emerging Euro Corps affords the EU the means to undertake such a role, one recently begun in Macedonia. Bosnia will follow shortly. We should make our complimentary strengths an asset, not a liability.

But too stark a division of labor is unhealthy. Europe must share more in the military aspect, and the U.S. share more in the peacekeeping and nation-building. For instance, Europe now provides the majority of troops and assistance in the Balkans and Afghanistan. In the future, we should allocate responsibilities before a crisis.

But this division of responsibilities will only work if Europe is made part of a shared process, so that the EU does not see itself as merely cleaning up after America's unilateral actions. The Bush administration will have to be more sensitive to European views, consult earlier, and try harder to reach a consensus on threats and their resolution. Europe must be part of the takeoffs, not just the crash landings.

The Administration is paying a stiff price for unilateralism by assuming greater burdens on American soldiers and taxpayers. Iraq was not an isolated incident, e.g., the withdrawal from the Kyoto Protocol, ABM Treaty, Small Arms Treaty, International Court Commissions, and the Landmines Treaty. But Europe must be ready to do its part. To repair our tattered European alliances, to act multilaterally whenever possible, the U.S. should develop an intensive dialogue regarding a shared approach to risks and ways to deal with them. But this will call for reciprocal action by Europe. The U.S. can do more to foster international consensus, but Europe must also help to achieve it. The defense budgets of most of our NATO allies are declining at a time when they should be increasing. NATO must act in Iraq as it is now doing in Afghanistan. The EU's Common Foreign and Security Policy, to be strengthened by the new EU Constitution and a single foreign minister, must make the EU a real partner with the U.S. in building a more stable world. The Euro Corps will have to move from the realm of ideas into that of reality, and be a part of the NATO organization.

There are some signs that both sides are trying to heal the rift. The Administration is seeking UN, EU, and NATO help in Iraq. Europe is recognizing its responsibilities in an era of terrorism that has now struck the European continent and threatens its safety and values as it does ours. Under the leadership of Javier Solana, the European Council has taken a more robust position against the threat of WMD. The British, French, and Germans have shown a united front in demanding that Iran open itself to the full scope of nuclear inspections by the IAEA as a condition of improved trade relations. Europe has been supportive of the Administration's diplomatic, multilateral approach to dealing with the North Korean nuclear threat. The French-Belgian effort to build a common defense independent of NATO has collapsed. The EU has declared Hamas' civilian, as well as military wing, a terrorist organization. The countries of the EU have cooperated in the war against terrorism by freezing terrorist assets, breaking up terrorist cells, and sharing intelligence on terrorist groups. But most fundamentally, the states of the EU must continue to see the U.S. as an important presence in Europe and as its best partner. With the accession of the new Central European member states, the U.S. should not engage in a "divide and conquer" strategy with the EU. The U.S. should pledge in a new Atlantic Charter to support the EU's evolving Common Foreign and Security Policy. The EU, for its part, should pledge to use CFSP to work in partnership with the U.S. to solve world problems.

We need to seek ways to act jointly—to deal with the HIV/AIDS epidemic, to confront Russia regarding breaches of the rule of law, to stop genocide in the Sudan. We should pledge to elevate our political relations with the EU to a level at least comparable to former relations with the most important EU member states and clearly support deeper enterprises. But this will require the EU to act more coherently, so the U.S. can deal with it affirmatively.

Fourth, we should have a private sector component in the new Atlantic Charter—as we do in the new transatlantic agenda. This would foster and strengthen transatlantic dialogue between businesses and environmental, labor, corporate, and activist groups. More exchanges among people in the nongovernmental sector will promote shared values and common purposes.

Virtually every major challenge facing the U.S. and Europe, from preventing genocides (in Bosnia and Kosovo) to increasing world trade, to confronting global environmental dangers, to dealing with HIV/AIDS, to eliminating threats, to human rights to drug trafficking, to terrorism and to threats of WMD, requires our coordinated action as genuine partners. United we can make the world more safe, stable, democratic, and prosperous. We can spread the benefits of democracy, the rule of law, and free market economies to the rest of the world.[1]

## Note

1. This paper has benefited from reports by two groups of which I am a member: the Council on Foreign Relations Task Force on "Renewing the Atlantic Partnership" (2004), coauthored by Henry Kissinger and Lawrence Summers, and a CSIS group which issued a Joint Declaration on "Renewing the Transatlantic Relationship" (2003).

# The Honorable Jans Held Madsen

## Chairman, Parliament Foreign Affairs Committee of Denmark

C AN THE POLITICAL AND MILITARY TENSIONS between the U.S. and Europe lead to a disruption of economic relations? I could start by saying "no," because from a historical point of view, we are so connected to each other that such a development is nearly impossible. Yet there are developments underway in Europe and the United States that are taking us in different directions.

Let me start with Europe. I see a change in structure, as it tries to become a "new Europe" and develop an identity as an independent actor with its own priorities. The European community has developed impressively since its founding in the early 1950s. The end of the Cold War led to the development of the Maastricht Treaty and the single European currency.

All that is a matter of building more coordination in Europe. And there can be no coordination if we do not have some kind of organization to take care of foreign policy and security policy. Many have said that the European Union is not democratic. I beg to differ. If you look at all the discussion and debate going on in the EU, it actually shows how democratic the whole project is. It shows the EU to be a cooperation between independent national states with their own sovereignty, but still looking for their own identity as "Europe."

Second, we have to be very aware that the postwar generation in Europe and the United States is actually ceding the center stage to a new generation of politicians. This postwar generation, in my opinion, very much evolved their political opinions from the heritage of our world wars and the need for transatlantic cooperation. Now, a new generation, who when they were younger were very critical of some of the foreign and security policy in the

United States, is coming to power. This generation will not feel the same guilt from the Second World War, which will change attitudes toward allocating resources for future cooperation in foreign policy and security policy.

The third thing I want to mention is the democratic development in Europe. How are we going to take up the challenges of immigration and integration? How will we deal with people getting older with fewer younger people to support them? Some projections indicate that by 2030, basic pension payments and increased health care costs for the elderly will put net governmental financial liabilities in Germany, France, Italy, and Spain at close to 200 percent of GDP.

I mention these issues because the welfare states built up in Europe will face a huge challenge in the future. If we do not have political leadership who have the will to tell the population that it cannot continue in this fashion, there will actually be fewer resources for cooperative security and foreign policy.

There is also a major change in the United States resulting from 9/11. You can see a different level of concern about terrorism. As a result, there has been a lot of misunderstanding in the dialogue between the United States and Europe. On the European side, right or wrong, there is not the same level of fear of terrorism.

The challenge is that we must not forget our history. I am concerned that the new politicians, especially in Europe, are forgetting the tremendous cooperation and also the help that we have gotten from the United States in very difficult times.

The challenge for the United States is not to forget the power of multilateral cooperation. We cannot have a superpower, whose foreign policy is actually making global foreign policy, reflect only what is going on domestically in the United States. Europe will not accept that. The United States will also have to be very aware that Europe cannot always be the guys who clean up after a war by civilian help and development aid and so on.

Europe's challenge is that they have to recognize that terror is also Europe's problem; in fact, the whole world's problem. They have to use more resources and develop a better understanding of the United States on the issue of terror. I feel Europe has a great challenge of living up to its responsibility and showing the gratitude that we surely have to the United States, from a historical sense.

# The Honorable Barbara McDougall

## Former Minister of Foreign Affairs of Canada

I WAS INTERESTED THAT MR. EIZENSTAT TALKED about a new Transatlantic Charter, because if you look back to the institutions, and particularly the economic institutions, that were created at the end of World War II, they were created, essentially, jointly by Europe and the United States and Canada. But they were created by people who were, as one of our economists says, "walking backwards." The purpose of setting up these institutions was to deal with the problems that developed in the 1930s: depression and deflation and unemployment. They were not created with a forward-looking view to what problems might come in the future.

Having said that, they have worked remarkably well. One of the great benefits has been the deep and broad, integrated economies that Europe and North America have. With Europe expanding by another ten members, that provides a basis for even further growth and integration in the years ahead.

Canada is the largest single-country trading partner of the U.S. The European Union is Canada's second largest market, if taken as a whole, and we are the twelfth market for the EU. That is in trade only; none of these numbers include foreign direct investment (FDI) or financial flows.

The EU and U.S. comprise about a fifth of each other's trade. They are the largest global traders, while Canada, with a population of 30 million, is fifth.

The EU is in a position right now where it desperately needs economic growth. It has been essentially stalled for several years. It is the laggard of the world economic boom, and that creates problems for the partnership and the trading relationship between North America and Europe. On the other hand, the U.S. faces a problem with its fiscal situation, which is very close to being out of control and is causing worries to U.S. economists. These two challenges threaten trade and economic relationships maybe even more than political tensions do.

There is no financial evidence that the political tensions between Europe and the U.S. has been translated into economic tension. If you look at FDI in the U.S., in 2003 it more than doubled to $72 billion, and most of that growth came from investment from Europe. That suggests to me a thriving economic and business relationship.

But there is a difference between government economic activity—which incorporates procurement and defense, for example—and the private sector. So far, there is no evidence of a decline in activity in the relationship in either the private or the public sectors. In the private sector, there are so many players that it would be almost impossible to contemplate a decline in activity that was caused by noneconomic or nonbusiness factors other than, of course, any potentially negative international agreements that are signed. But the private sector will make decisions based less on political tensions than on business conditions and business outlook and corporate objectives. If there were an effort to contain financial flows for political reasons, it would cause huge economic damage.

At the end of June, the EU and the U.S. held their annual economic summit. This is one of those summits that is held every year and sometimes produces something, but usually does not. What the parties did do this year was to refresh their commitment to joint growth and support. They talked specifically about cooperation on the Doha Round and financial market regulation.

These are all noises that one would expect, and that is encouraging. I was concerned there would be an impact on multilateral trading negotiations as a result of the tension, but I do not see the evidence of that, at least not yet. This is very important. There must be joint action on multilateral issues. Cotton subsidies, for example, are devastating African farmers. We have to come to grips with such problems, and we can only do so in multilateral trade settings.

We have to look forward. We have to build institutions that will enhance our growth and our capacity to cooperate. We face common problems like aging populations, which will have a huge economic impact. The evidence suggests that we are going to continue to be able to do so.

# Dr. Richard Rahn

## Former Chief Economist,
## United States Chamber of Commerce

WHAT I HAVE BEEN DOING IN THE LAST FEW YEARS is primarily working with Europeans to help build think tanks in the way that we have here, such as the Brookings Institution, AEI, Heritage, Cato, and so forth. The Europeans have lagged behind in development of think tanks, which add a lot to national dialogue.

I do not see a major problem between the U.S. and Europe as a result of political-military tensions. What I do see, though, is a major European problem: the demographic crisis. In Italy, for example, you have only 1.2 children per woman, while you need a rate of 2.1 for replacement. Britain, France, and Germany also are well below replacement level, as are several of the other European countries.

This low birthrate, coupled with the early retirement ages in some of these countries and extensive social welfare benefits, is a really serious crisis. People in the United States are concerned about Social Security, but our problems are easily solved compared to what the Europeans are facing. And this crisis in the European economies, primarily a result of increasing taxes and regulations and in part driven by these demographic problems, has serious ramifications for the U.S. and the rest of the world.

There has been a large outflow of capital from Europe into the U.S. Most of this capital is flowing out of France and Germany, some out of Italy. Britain is still a capital importing country, Ireland is a capital importing country, and the new nations of the former communist bloc which have joined the EU are primarily capital importers.

The big capital exporters have not acted in what I consider a rational way. They have been pushing such things as the European Savings Directive, which is an attempt to try to stem capital outflow by requiring reporting from neighboring countries about Europeans who have moved their savings to Switzerland or Luxembourg or Austria or Britain or the U.S. or wherever. Now, the European Savings Directive has both been delayed and so watered down as to be meaningless from an economic standpoint, and there are endless ways to get around it. But its very existence acknowledges that there is a problem. It is an irrational solution to the underlying problem. There was a very interesting study done by the National Bureau of Economic Researchers there this past year showing that attempts to curtail outflows of capital are even damaging Britain and France.

The correct solution, of course, is to reduce taxes and to make themselves more tax competitive. You have the attempts by, in particular, Germany and France for what they call tax harmonization. At the same time, we have seen the new entrants into Europe come down with flat taxes and lower corporate rates. The lowest corporate rate in Europe is in Ireland: 12.5 percent. The new entrants have corporate tax rates in the 15 percent range.

This is necessary for them to grow and to attract capital. When the Germans and the French say these countries have got to get taxes up to their levels, they are basically taking away a lot of the competitive advantage that the new countries need to get their economies growing at a more rapid rate and bring capital incomes up. The same thing is true with the extension of some of the labor rules that France and Germany have and are trying to impose on the new entrants. If you take away all of the competitive advantages for the new entrants, they will always remain far behind, and that is undesirable.

The U.S. has not been as strong as I would like to see in supporting pro-growth policies, primarily in the countries in Central and Eastern Europe, Ireland, and some other regions. There was an interest-reporting regulation promulgated at the end of the Clinton administration, but never actually published. The Bush administration has left it out there, in part to keep France and Germany happy. But it is dangerous to us, because we need those capital inflows to maintain our rate of growth.

Often, people look at the trade deficit in a rather backwards way. They say: "We are being damaged by the trade deficit." Actually, it is the demand for investment in the U.S. which causes the trade deficit. You find that more rapidly developing economies tend to have trade deficits and that stagnant or slow growth economies, like Japan, Germany, and France, run the big trade surpluses.

On another aspect, I would take issue with Minister McDougall. The U.S. is not in a fiscal crisis. Our debt-to-GDP ratio is about 35 or 36 percent, much lower than that of the European countries. Japan's debt-to-GDP ratio is over 100 percent now. Our debt-to-GDP ratio is actually near its record low for the post–World War II era. At the end of World War II it was 128 percent. We borrowed to win World War II. In 1960, it was almost 50 percent. It slowly has come down as a result of economic growth.

Obviously, you cannot run fiscal deficits of more than 2 to 3 percent or that ratio increases. Having gone into a recession, it was appropriate for us to run a deficit. I was not happy with the growth in spending, but the deficit is not particularly damaging, provided we get it back down in the next two to three years to the 2 to 3 percent level. We could run a 2 percent deficit forever if we had growth rates of 3.5 to 4 percent in our economy, and that GDP-to-debt ratio would never increase.

I would be much more concerned if I were Italian or Japanese or French or German. In Germany now, looking at their debt-to-GDP ratio, the situation is far more serious than here in the U.S. My view is that the U.S. ought to do much more to encourage pro-growth policies in Europe. The fact that Europe has been falling behind the U.S. in economic growth leads to tensions.

I am one of those who believes that we want all of the world rich. You do not have trouble with rich neighbors. One reason we have very few problems with Canada is because we are both wealthy. We have problems with Mexico primarily because of the income differentials. High growth in the poorer countries is the only way to world peace, in my judgment. It is also the humane thing. I want us to encourage those policies that bring high growth, i.e., the rule of law, nondestructive tax and regulatory systems, and free trade.

# II

# Under What Conditions Is a Transatlantic Political Consensus on the Use of Force Possible?

# The Honorable Curt Weldon

Member, United States House of Representatives
(R-PA); Vice Chairman, House of Representatives
Committee on Armed Services

MY PERSPECTIVE IS FROM THE U.S. CONGRESS, as someone who has been on the Armed Services Committee for eighteen years working issues involving our national security. During that time, I have spent a good deal of effort reaching out to the former Soviet states. I have traveled there some thirty-seven times, and formed and chaired the Interparliamentary Dialogue with the Russian Duma. I have had excellent relations with members of the European parliaments and various individuals in Europe, but have been concerned about our relations as of late.

My ultimate responsibility in Congress, besides protecting our military, is to avoid war. War is an indication of failure—a situation where we have not exercised diplomacy aggressively enough to try to find ways to take adversaries or would-be adversaries and turn them into, if not partners, then at least countries that we can work with to resolve problems and conflicts peacefully.

I found it very frustrating when the U.S. and other European countries got involved in the invasion of the former Yugoslavia to remove Milosevic. It was not that anyone in America thought that Milosevic was anything other than a war criminal. But the concern that we had in the United States was that the Administration was taking an approach to resolve that conflict without allowing Russia to play a role in using her influence—and actually, in some cases, forcing Russia to play a more aggressive role. Knowing full well that Russia would have vetoed a United Nations resolution, the European community, largely led by France and Germany, coupled with the U.S., avoided the UN and instead used NATO.

As we all know, NATO was designed to be a defensive organization. Many of my colleagues, as well as I myself, therefore felt that the Balkan war was a bad precedent, because it was the first and only time that NATO was used in an offensive role to invade a non-NATO country.

In fact, I took an eleven-member congressional delegation to Vienna. Five Democrats and five Republicans met with the leaders of all political factions from Russia, including the deputy chairman of the Communist faction, the leader of the "Yedinstvo" faction, which is the party of Boris Yeltsin, and Viktor Chernomyrdin, leader of the "Yabloko" faction, and several others. Over two days, we reached an understanding with the Russians that led to what became the G-8 agreement to end the war.

The case of Iraq was very divisive. In Yugoslavia, we set a precedent by using military force through NATO without going through the UN. In Iraq, there were seventeen UN resolutions. Saddam did not comply with the terms of the settlement after the Gulf War in the early 1990s. So there was a disheartened feeling in the United States Congress that perhaps there was a double standard.

Now, perhaps that is not the case. We can talk to our European friends and understand that there were legitimate reasons why they did not think war against Iraq was the right approach to take. Be that as it may, we now have to worry about the future and how to work together.

I am not a diplomat, nor do I ever hope to be one. I love my job as a parliamentarian. And I believe part of the solution lies in establishing more aggressive relationships at the parliamentary level and understanding that diplomacy has always got to be pushed to the limits.

I have set up eight interparliamentary dialogues, including ones with the Ukrainian Rada, the Moldavian Parliament, the Modulus in Azerbaijan, and the Modulus in Uzbekistan. By setting up these interparliamentary dialogues, we build trust and confidence that can perhaps help our governments to avoid violence and military conflict when situations arise.

I cannot speak as a leader of the Administration, because I am not. Nor am I someone speaking on behalf of our government. But in terms of the role that the U.S. *can* play, it is critically important that we, over the next twenty-five years, support, enhance, and grow parliamentary relationships.

I think back to my earlier contacts with Russia. The first delegation I hosted in my congressional district in 1985 was made up of twelve young communists. It was a very untimely thing for me to do as a conservative Republican in a Republican suburb of Philadelphia, and I took a lot of heat for that. Well, today, one of those delegates, Valentina Matvienko, is the governor of Saint Petersburg. Another of those delegates is now the Deputy Provost of MGIMO, the most prestigious educational institution in Moscow, training the diplomatic corps and the leaders of foreign policy. All of the contacts we made back then are extremely important today in helping our respective administrations find means outside of war to resolve conflict.

I therefore look at our efforts in Europe and the newly emerging Europe and think about our ability to reach out to people like Aleksandr Lukashenko. I took a delegation to Minsk and had the opportunity to speak with him about the problems and difficulties Belarus faces with the OSCE. We stressed the importance of taking certain steps to rejoin the family of nations. We did the same with Leonid Kuchma in Ukraine, back when Kuchma was wondering whether or not he should support the effort against terrorism and whether or not he should ratify the U.S. choice to represent the OSCE. Eventually, Kuchma came around and supported all of those activities.

In short, there is a role for us as parliamentarians to play that runs parallel to the efforts of our governments. We have to renew, enhance, and increase the relationships between the parliaments. I am convinced that there are no problems that we cannot solve, and no issues that we cannot resolve.

The other areas we should be focusing on are two major issues that may allow disparate countries to come together. The first is energy. Last year, we formed the International Energy Advisory Council, which is made up of private-sector energy interests from around the world. We have now had four sessions. The fifth one will take place in Yalta, focusing on Europe's energy needs, and how we can work together. Energy can bring countries together. Energy can help resolve conflict.

The second is the oceans. This is the year of the oceans in America. We have released our second Oceans Commission report, working together with the Advisory Council on Protecting the Seas, a London-based consortium made up of thirty-five nations of parliamentarians and administrative-level officials. We can find a common agenda that brings countries together to resolve conflict, not just in Europe but also in neighboring countries in Africa, in the Middle East, and the Far East.

To do so, we need to reinforce the role of our parliamentarians.

# The Honorable Lothar Binding

## Member of the Deutsche Bundestag, Germany

THE WAY THIS QUESTION IS FORMULATED ASSUMES that there is a set of conditions that, once they are met, create a transatlantic political consensus. But this set of conditions does not exist.

Comparing the situations, background, and information concerning Yugoslavia, Afghanistan, or Iraq, we find a wide variety of goals, reactions, and types of engagement between different governments, as well as major differences in the way the UN, NATO, and the different countries of Europe took part in solving these conflicts.

The most recent war in Iraq clearly revealed the obstacles we have to overcome in relation to transatlantic cooperation. There was tension between certain European nations and the U.S., but there were also tensions among European nations. If we look more closely, there were also differences of opinion within the United States, between the peace movement and the government, for example, just as there were differences of opinion in Germany between the opposition and the government.

It is easy to see how complex the question of "objective differences in national interests between the U.S. and Europe" is, and to realize that the question really has to remain unanswered for as long as we in Europe are unable to agree on a truly common foreign and security policy. Even the European Constitution does not provide an adequate basis for this process.

These tensions arise from the fact that political goals are often defined on a day-to-day basis: sometimes according to strategic considerations, sometimes in order to secure influence with respect to certain mineral resources, and, in the worst case, also to divert attention from problems on the domestic front.

To this extent, national interests are frequently not in accord with the goals that all people share, and moral and ethical categories that are important to all of us are pushed into the background. This is why we need a new dimension as we seek to achieve a European, and then also a transatlantic, consensus. Central to these efforts are moves to democratize and strengthen the UN and to improve the intergovernmental consultation process.

With this in mind, I would like to refer to the Transatlantic Policy Network report[1] as a basis for a new political consensus. That study says that, from a political point of view, we have to build a transatlantic community for regional and global cooperation, founded on:

- Peace, democracy, and development in the extended Middle East
- The fight against terrorism
- Curbing the proliferation of weapons of mass destruction
- Fighting AIDS and infectious diseases
- The long-term integration of China into the global community
- The further transformation of Russia and other countries into democratic states, market economies and strategic partners

We will have to deepen practical cooperation on energy and climate change and stimulate the constructive involvement of relevant communities of interest from American and European civil society in collaborative activities regarding transatlantic partnership priorities. And, in order to improve the interparliamentary dialogue, we should strengthen the institutional structure for an ongoing transatlantic political dialogue (the TLD, or Transatlantic Legislators Dialogue).

From an economic point of view, we have to deepen and broaden the transatlantic market for financial services and capital markets; civil aviation; the digital economy (privacy, security, and intellectual property rights); competition policy, and; regulatory cooperation. We also will have to strengthen transatlantic economic and monetary cooperation and revitalize WTO negotiations.

Concerning defense and security, we should promote more open transatlantic defense markets and closer cooperation between transatlantic defense industries, further develop the NATO/EU interface and, most importantly, develop a framework for a broader permanent EU-U.S. security dialogue—the kind of dialogue that did not exist after September 11th and before the war in Iraq.

These few remarks provide a glimpse into how I would answer the question: "Under what conditions is a transatlantic political consensus possible?" Looking at this question abstractly, it is indeed possible, without reference to nations or peoples, to define quite quickly a list of common views and common goals that describe the transatlantic political consensus. They are:

- Peace throughout the world
- The eradication of poverty
- The ability to live in security and without fear of the future
- A fair distribution of work and income
- Equality of opportunities, social justice
- Education for all, access to the benefits of innovations
- The restoration of an intact environment
- Cross-generational (sustainable) policies for humans and the environment

## Note

1. *A Strategy to Strengthen Transatlantic Partnership*, Report of the Transatlantic Policy Network, December 4, 2003, www.tpnonline.org/031203Communique.pdf.

# Dr. John Lenczowski

## Director, Institute of
## World Politics, Washington, D.C.

I VERY MUCH SUBSCRIBE TO MANY of the points previous speakers have made concerning the importance of dialogue and diplomacy in U.S.-European relations. I also agree with Mr. Binding that it is difficult to come up with a set of a priori conditions of where political consensus can be achieved concerning the use of force because of the unique character of almost each situation.

The real strategic problem is not so much establishing consensus on when to use force, but rather how to succeed in defending our respective national interests while minimizing the necessity of having to use force. I happen to be one of those who believe that the U.S. use of force in Iraq was one where an insufficient case was made by our government to demonstrate why, indeed, this was truly a last resort.

Accordingly, I believe that some European hesitations can be well understood. But Europe has to understand that the recent use of force by the United States is very much a function of a longstanding disinvestment in public diplomacy and in certain types of intelligence and defense preparations.

In order to prevent many different kinds of conflicts, and in order to avoid certain types of aggression, you need to have a credible defense posture. Such a posture is, first and foremost, politically based. Ultimately, however, you have to have strong armed forces, strong anti-terrorist special forces and a strong covert action capability. And you must have credibility when it comes to such things as deterrence.

The United States has been extremely inconsistent over the last decade concerning these matters. We maintain strong conventional forces, but there was a perception amongst Islamist extremists that the United States was weak, soft, inconstant and, therefore, vulnerable to terrorist acts. Fortunately, the United States has a large constituency that is in favor of restoring these types of capabilities.

In Europe, on the other hand, that constituency is a very small one. Europe has been failing in its ability to project a credible deterrent—specifically, counterterrorist capabilities. The Islamic world considers Europe to be even softer and weaker than the United States; both materialistic and hedonistic. Ultimately, of course, this is a larger cultural and civilizational issue; one cannot have strategic means without strategy, and one cannot have strategy without coherent national security and foreign policy goals, and one cannot have such goals unless one has a consensus of values particularly rooted in a zealous desire to protect a civilization.

What I do not see in Europe is any kind of manifest desire to protect the respective civilizations of the various nations, except, perhaps in the so-called New Europe, where there has been an attempt by many countries to build free societies as they emerge from the oppression under which they had to live for so long.

This gets down to a question of the degree to which Europe is serious about security goals and serious about defending its civilization. We in America see a Europe that is committing demographic suicide, that is gradually becoming more Muslim, and that somehow does not seem serious about doing its part to defending civilization in a way that would minimize the necessity of using coercive means.

Many Europeans have legitimate concerns about the American willingness to use force more as a first resort than a last resort. I think we were mistaken to put forth a doctrine of preemption because, if it is necessary to preempt, one should just go ahead and do so without enshrining it provocatively as a doctrine. But I also believe that the question of preemption is widely understood in Europe as something that has to meet the conditions of "just war" doctrine, where preemption is justified because there is 100 percent certainty of imminent attack. This was not the case in the Iraq situation.

In any event, greater sensitivity on our part is merited, and will need to develop if we are to continue the kind of transatlantic dialogue which we used to have, where differences of opinion can be shared in a civilized manner.

# III

# What Role Has the Media Played in U.S.-European Relations?

# Martin Walker

## Editor-in-Chief, United Press International

POLITICIANS OFTEN FIND IT CONVENIENT to blame the messenger, but there is a lot of blame to be shared for the transatlantic tirades that have marked the long crisis in EU-U.S. relations. The prize might go to Jonah Goldberg of *National Review*, who first borrowed from the Simpsons cartoons to popularize the phrase "cheese-eating surrender monkeys" to describe the French. Some of the humor was rather more pointed, like the joke in George Will's *Newsweek* column: "How many Frenchmen does it take to defend Paris? No one knows, it's never been tried." (Not true. Paris held out against the German armies in the famous siege of 1870–1871, and was defended to considerable effect from 1914–1918.)

But the jokes kept on coming, on TV as well as in the press. Regis Philbin suggested that "The only time France wants us to go to war is when the German Army is sitting in Paris sipping coffee." He paused for laughs, and then went on: "Next time there's a war in Europe, the loser has to keep France." Jay Leno chimed in with "I don't know why people are surprised that France won't help us get Saddam out of Iraq. After all, France wouldn't help us get the Germans out of France!"

I'm afraid I could not resist the temptation to join in, asking the famous question that has intrigued tourists for decades: "Why did the French plant those elegant avenues of trees alongside their long, straight country roads? So that the German army could march in the shade."

Jokes, even insulting ones, are one thing. But it is much more sobering when a serious and respected newspaper casts into doubt the whole basis of the Atlantic Alliance, like the *Wall Street Journal Europe* did in an editorial on June 28th of this year:

> NATO's European leaders will congratulate each other for agreeing to train Iraqi security services, a job France and Germany somehow intend to accomplish without sending any troops to Iraq. If that's all the help the U.S. can get from our partners, it may be time to rethink the underlying premise of this "alliance."
>
> Earlier this month, the U.S. and Europe commemorated the sacrifices of American soldiers on the Normandy beaches. For the next 60 years, American taxpayers footed most of the bill to protect Europe. Europeans appear to believe Americans will continue doing this indefinitely, regardless of European behavior. They are badly mistaken.

This was not simply an American view. The previous day, Germany's *Süddeutsche Zeitung* (June 27) had run an editorial that read:

> George Bush and Tony Blair, and Gerhard Schröder and Jacques Chirac, are stage-managing harmony. With a few decisions on Iraq, the Balkans and Afghanistan they want to and have to give the impression NATO is going strong. But it's all a whitewash. They might be able to disguise the splits in the alliance until the U.S. elections. But by the end of the year at the latest, all the tensions pulling at the alliance from within will burst through.
>
> Many EU governments are wary of telling their people what is in store: more money for international troop deployments, more danger far from home and more deaths. The new transatlantic unity is a fairy tale.

Again, June 28th, this time from William Safire's august perch on the Op-Ed page of the *New York Times*:

> Mr. Bush and Mr. Blair can face elections this year and next, able to make two claims: that the prewar split in the western alliance has happily healed, and that the war was justified by the belated blessing of the leaders who fled from the fight. Behind this facade, however, exists a hollowed-out alliance. Its previous common purpose—to block the westward march of Soviet imperialism—has not been replaced by a new purpose: to defeat imperial terrorism. Unless the democracies of France and Germany elect leaders capable of grasping that current challenge, NATO will continue to atrophy, supplanted by ad hoc coalitions of the willing to meet emergencies.

And giving equal time to the Europeans, the *Financial Times* editorial of the same day said:

> NATO looks like it is becoming an increasingly European (and Canadian) alliance, if the U.S. prefers for military reasons to operate on its own, or is con-

demned to do so for political reasons. NATO failure in Afghanistan would therefore not only rock Europe's alliance with the U.S., but also throw into question its readiness to mount any far-flung military operations, even under an EU banner. The only residual role for NATO would be to provide extra security, as it is doing this summer, for events such as the Athens Olympics.

This is getting serious. It is one thing when a tabloid paper like Rupert Murdoch's *New York Post* portrays the French and Germans at the UN as an "axis of weasels," as it did in February of last year. Or, when it shows the graves of Normandy with the headline: "They died for France but France has forgotten." A cartoon in the same paper shows an ostrich with its head in the sand below the words: "The national bird of France." This is the Murdoch press, whose sister paper in Britain, *The Sun*, routinely reports every England-Germany soccer match as a replay of World War II, and which invited its readers to turn to the East and shout as one "Sod off, you Frogs," and which celebrated the sinking of an Argentine battleship and the loss of over five hundred lives with the famous headline "Gotcha!" The Murdoch press revels in its mastery of journalism as vaudeville. But it gets more serious when serious papers take up the same theme.

In the *Wall Street Journal*, Christopher Hitchens described Jacques Chirac as "a positive monster of conceit—the abject procurer for Saddam . . . the rat that tried to roar."

In the *Washington Post*, George Will opined that the "oily" foreign affairs minister, Dominique de Villepin, had launched France into "an exercise for which France has often refined its *savoir-faire* since 1870, which is to say retreat—this time into incoherence."

And in the *New York Times*, Thomas Friedman argued that France should be removed from the Security Council and be replaced with India: "India is just so much more serious than France these days. France is so caught up with its need to differentiate itself from America to feel important, it's become silly."

The *Wall Street Journal* editor, Max Boot, argues: "France has been in decline since, oh, about 1815, and it isn't happy about it. What particularly galls the Gauls is that their rightful place in the world has been usurped by the gauche Americans."

At its ugliest, the transatlantic bile is becoming increasingly personal. When France Interradio's correspondent in Washington, Laurence Simon, started to explain her government's position to *Fox News* (owned by Murdoch), she was interrupted by the presenter. "With friends like you, who needs enemies," she was told as she was taken off air.

So this is not just a matter of tabloid newspapers or even tabloid TV. Serious commentators from both sides of the Atlantic were reflecting a mutual antagonism and a growing doubt about the Alliance's future. Even those most committed to the NATO alliance were warning of its peril. Take, for example, Sir Max Hastings, a historian and former editor of both the *Daily Telegraph* and the *Evening Standard*, writing in the *Guardian* newspaper on April 24th of this year:

> What we really need to debate is the issue of how the world manages the United States, the world's only superpower. The matter of Iraq will some day be resolved, however unsatisfactorily. It will fade from the headlines. But the matter of America will not go away. Somehow, the world, in general, and the British, in particular, have to consider anew our relationship with the power of the U.S. granted the less-than-godlike nature of most of the presidents elected to exercise it. . . . Britain's defence policy today rests on the avowed presumption that we shall never have to engage in conflict without the Americans. This may represent reality, but it is also a huge European abdication of responsibility. If we are really fed up with Bush, if we recognize that no future U.S. president is likely to be entirely to our taste, we should surely get on with creating credible European armed forces. As it is, no European nation—with the possible exception of France—shows the smallest interest in spending money or displaying spine for this purpose.
>
> Until we address this, and against the background of a struggle against international terrorism that is likely to grow more alarming rather than less, America remains the indispensable ally and shield. That means George Bush. At the very moment when most of us feel surfeited with the president's vacuous grin and impregnable moral conceit, we cannot walk away from his follies unless or until Europe makes itself something quite different from the eunuch it is today.

That was Max being mild. In another column, he really told us what he thought, under the headline "I hate George Bush": "It is hard not to hate George Bush. His ignorance and conceit, his professed special relationship with God, invite revulsion."

Hastings is right. This is not just a matter of Iraq. Some of this media gloom-and-doom, it should be remembered, predates the arguments over the Iraq war. A year before Baghdad fell, Charles Krauthammer in the *Washington Post* was diagnosing a new sickness across the Atlantic:

> In Europe, it is not very safe to be a Jew. How could this be? The explanation is not that difficult to find. What we are seeing is pent-up anti-Semitism, the release—with Israel as the trigger—of a millennium-old urge that powerfully infected and shaped European history. What is odd is not the anti-Semitism of today, but its relative absence during the last half-century. That was the historical anomaly. Holocaust shame kept the demon corked for that half-century. But now the atonement is passed. The genie is out again.

This time, however, it is more sophisticated. It is not a blanket hatred of Jews. Jews can be tolerated, even accepted, but they must know their place. Jews are fine so long as they are powerless, passive and picturesque. What is intolerable is Jewish assertiveness, the Jewish refusal to accept victimhood. And nothing so embodies that as the Jewish state.

What so offends Europeans is the armed Jew, the Jew who refuses to sustain seven suicide bombings in the seven days of Passover and strikes back. That Jew has been demonized in the European press as never before since, well . . . since the '30s. The liberal Italian daily *La Stampa* ran a cartoon of the baby Jesus, besieged by Israeli tanks, saying, "Don't tell me they want to kill me again."

Well, that is just one theme, albeit about as ugly a charge as can be leveled. But there was a more general malaise long before. In President Bush's first year in office, the Europeans were already making it clear that he was less than welcome.

*The Guardian* (liberal), June 19, 2001:

Europeans can indeed now see Mr. Bush for what he is: the affable, inflexible frontman for a right-wing business, political, and military alliance intent on pursuing the logic of solo superpower to its domineering conclusion. This administration really does seem to believe it can have it all. Perhaps, in time, it will learn differently—for Mr. Bush's simplistic, lopsided global view conceals a basic lack of common sense and understanding.

But the *Guardian* went on to sound a note of thoughtful caution: "We are moving into a very dangerous period in the Atlantic relationship, as the United States looks increasingly west and Europe increasingly east. It will be all too easy to let these tensions degenerate into a popular mood which is dismissive and impatient with Europe on the U.S. side of the Atlantic and slips into raw anti-Americanism on ours. All too easy—but profoundly dangerous."

France's *Le Figaro* that summer coined the famous phrase "the toxic Texan" for the visiting new president, and these jibes worried some other Europeans, new to the rough-and-tumble of transatlantic relations.

From Poland's *Wprost* (weekly newsmagazine), June 24, 2001:

[The European] approach to the new president is schizophrenic. On one hand, Europeans accuse his administration of being too self-centered, and on the other, they accuse him of playing the global bully. France, always ready to complain about America, has called the U.S. a hyper-power. In Poland, Western Europe's anti-Americanism seems incomprehensible. Why this allergic reaction to Bush? It's simple: the leftist establishment in most European countries hates him. How not to hate someone who thinks that the state is the source of problems instead of an aid in solving them, who is not obsessed with ecology, who calls himself a born-again Christian, and who, when asked who has had the biggest influence on his life, unhesitatingly responds, "Jesus Christ?" Bush has the misfortune that for the first time since the end of the cold war, the Right rules America and the Left rules the majority of European countries.

Would that it were so simple. And would that moment of solidarity after 9/11 when France's *Le Monde* published its famous headline "We are all Americans now" had endured.

But we are where we are. And we are here not simply because of the media but because of the politicians—on both sides of the Atlantic. Jokes and commentaries aside, one job of the media is to report what the elected politicians say—and what they were saying long before the arguments over the Iraq war. The last French foreign minister, the Socialist Hubert Vedrine, who coined the term "hyperpuissance" to describe the U.S. superpower, enjoyed a long conversation with a group of foreign journalists last December in Paris. Discussing the European Union's plans to develop its own autonomous defense capability, he said: "In the American suspicion of European defense, there is an initial aspect which we can't accept, which has to be got over, and that is a sort of determination to be top dog."

Vedrine put this another way in a speech to French diplomats shortly after he took office in 1997. "There is only one great power nowadays, the United States, but unless it is counter-balanced, that power brings with it the risk of monopoly domination." His answer was to propose that France should take the lead in a European Union which "must gradually affirm itself as a centre of power."

This is not just a Socialist speaking. The current (and conservative) French foreign minister, Michel Barnier, in a seminar this summer, insisted, "What our American friends must understand is that we are going to build Europe not only as a market but as a power."

Nor is this just a matter of the French. Michael Steiner, the foreign policy adviser to Chancellor Gerhard Schröder, reacted angrily when the United States blocked the initial German candidate to be the new International Monetary Fund managing director. "We have discovered that the superpower sees its global role not only in the military area but also in setting the rules of globalization through the IMF," he said.

Even former British foreign minister Douglas Hurd, a devout Atlanticist, noted recently: "A valid Atlantic partnership cannot safely depend on a unique superpower on one side of the Atlantic, with an array of Europeans on the other side, strong in rhetoric, but chronically short of coherence and muscle. . . . To some extent, the Americans have us both ways. If Europe became strong and determined in defence matters, some Americans would use this as a reason for withdrawal from Europe. Yet the same lesson might be drawn if Europe continued as feckless and idle as many American commentators believe we are."

Iraq, of course, made everything worse. Chris Patten, the European Union's commissioner for external affairs and a lifelong Americanophile, was appalled by President Bush's "axis of evil," formulation. "I find it hard to believe that's a thought-through policy," Patten said, going on to warn that an "absolutist and simplistic" Bush administration was going into "unilateralist overdrive." French foreign minister Hubert Vedrine told reporters, "We are friends of the United States, we are friends of that people and we will remain so. But we are threatened today by a new simplism [sic] which consists in reducing everything to the war on terrorism. . . . Europeans are unanimous in not supporting the Middle East policy of the White House." German deputy foreign minister, Ludger Vollmer, stated, "We Europeans warn against [attacking Iraq]. There is no indication, no proof that Iraq is involved in the terrorism we have been talking about for the last few months . . . this terror argument cannot be used to legitimize old enmities."

Let us go back to the beginning. It was not journalists who began the "America from Mars, Europe from Venus" debate; it was the Pentagon's after-action report on Kosovo, which warned that the European NATO allies were less and less capable of functioning usefully alongside U.S. forces on the modern battlefield. It was not journalists, but NATO secretary general George Robertson who condemned the feebleness of the European NATO allies who had two million troops under arms but had to strain every nerve to put even 40,000 of them into the field. It was not journalists but the U.S. secretary of defense who drew the famous distinction between "Old" and "New" Europe, and made it clear which one he preferred. It was not journalists, but the president of France, who declared that in all circumstances France would cast its UN veto against war in Iraq. It was a journalist who coined the famous phrase that U.S. policy after the war was to "punish France, forgive Russia and ignore Germany," but he wrote it immediately after a long and detailed interview with Condoleezza Rice and there is little question but that the phrase was hers.

In short, the journalists were not making it up. They were, tabloids and broadsheets alike, late night comics and sober commentators, reflecting a political reality—and reflecting the opinion polls in their countries—which is sadly still with us, and taking unusual new forms. Most observers of transatlantic affairs have long comforted themselves that whatever the rhetoric of the politicians, the economic self-interest of the world's two richest entities would keep the show on the road. So it was startling to read in France's *Le Figaro*, amid the latest dollar-euro gyrations, a front-page headline that said: "War between Euro and Dollar Threatens Economic Recovery." "Washington's attitude in seemingly allowing the dollar to plunge," the newspaper went on, "is crippling Europe, whose export industries are being penalized as a result."

And Secretary Rumsfeld's division of "Old" and "New" Europe may not be quite as clear as he would like. Slovakia's *Pravda* is not the only paper from the "New" Europe to take exception to what it sees as U.S. arrogance. But an editorial last month was striking in its critique: "So far, it would seem from America's behavior in Iraq that it can do more or less whatever it wants," *Pravda* said. "The road to hell is paved with good intentions, and Bush's road can also lead to hell."

I began these remarks with a phrase about shooting the messenger, so let me close with a tribute to a French colleague, Alain Hertoghe of *La Croix*, the Catholic daily. Last year, he published a book titled *La guerre à outrances* (War to the Death), and subtitled *How the press disinformed us on Iraq*. He argued, with solid sourcing, that the mainstream French press had reported the war they wanted to happen, a Vietnam-style quagmire—rather than the one that did. He analyzed the headlines in the five main French newspapers, *Le Monde*, *Le Figaro*, *Ouest-France*, *Liberation*, and *La Croix*, and found 135 negative ones on Bush and Blair, and only 35 negative ones on Saddam Hussein.

"The reporting, when it was uncertain what was going on, fell into predictions of disaster because there were so many who wanted everything to go wrong," Hertoghe wrote. "*Le Monde* became Saddam's gazette. It gave a picture from Baghdad of Saddam's units perfectly controlling the situation. Then when the Americans made their move, we read how they were massacring the Iraqis."

Alain Hertoghe was fired when the book appeared, for damaging the reputation of his newspaper and the authority of its chief editors and questioning the professional ethics of colleagues. Sometimes the messengers really do get shot.

# Georg Schmolz

## Correspondent, ARD Television, Germany

THE ROLE OF THE MEDIA BEFORE THE WAR in Iraq essentially came down to a problem of media image and of wrongly chosen strategy. If you take the example in Germany of Chancellor Gerhard Schröder, he was known, at the time, as what we call a "media chancellor"—always present when the media was present. If there was a camera—for example, at a TV game show—he was seen. During the flooding in eastern Germany, he was a very early presence.

When he declared during the election campaign that Germany was not going to support the U.S., it was a little bit surprising. And he did it in such a firm way that it became very difficult for him to get down off this monument he had himself erected.

In Washington, President George Bush was putting himself in a similar situation. He declared publicly that there had to be a war and that we would go into Iraq. It thus became difficult for him to withdraw in order to pursue a dialogue with those Europeans who hesitated to go to war. Even when Great Britain and France tried to find a way out of the situation with the United Nations, it was very difficult for, in this case, the American government and the German government to accept this way out.

Second, the arguments published in the European media regarding why war was necessary were not coherent. To express it a bit dramatically, every week there was another kind of argument about why it was necessary to go to Iraq. First, it was because George Bush Sr. didn't finish the job. Then, it was because there were weapons of mass destruction in Iraq. Then, it was the issue of how Saddam Hussein was behaving toward his people.

Thirdly, the coverage in Europe, particularly on the Continent (because Great Britain is definitely not the rule), was not centered on the question of what was going on in Iraq. Instead, it was much more focused on the question of what was going on among Europe, Germany, France, and the United States at the United Nations.

Another problem is that, to a large part of the population in Germany and in other European countries, this Iraq war was generally seen as unhelpful toward solving the problems of the Middle East as a whole. A lot of this had to do with particular points of view toward Israel and Palestinian people. Moreover, the media was much more occupied by questions such as: "Is Gerhard Schröder keeping his word?" and "Can he withstand the pressure from other governments, especially the pressure from Washington?"

Unlike the first Gulf War in the early 1990s, this one was waged without a country being occupied, and thus it would have been helpful to have some examples of why it was necessary to remove Saddam Hussein.

The problem was that no evidence was released or published. Whether this was a fault of the publications' editors or the result of a lack of information from the American government or British government or other governments, I cannot judge.

As you probably know, during the first Gulf War, the media described a very bad experience in which it was controlled and pictures were manipulated, which made journalists, especially in Europe, very, very careful about accepting information from official sources. It is a problem to give information during a time when information can easily be manipulated. The way the allied troops embedded the journalists was, at least in Germany, heavily criticized, because people were afraid that, again, it was an attempt to manipulate the journalists.

In the coverage of the war itself, there was an interesting paper released by a German media association called Media Tenua. They spent a fortnight at the end of March and the beginning of April comparing some of the German news programs with those of the BBC and ABC. Not surprisingly, the German coverage of the Iraqi people who suffered from the American and allied attacks was about 67 percent of all reports and just 29 percent treated casualties and problems of the allied troops. At ABC it was practically the reverse.

As we know today, the journalists probably did not manipulate the news in the sense that they knowingly gave the wrong information. But they probably had not checked their sources, which made things a little bit difficult.

Coming back to the theme of this conference, Iraq is probably one of the first visible problems in the German-central European-American relationship, and it did a lot of damage, in my opinion. Nevertheless, as Thomas Donnelly of the American Enterprise Institute mentioned a couple of weeks ago, America has to learn to live without Europe.

In my own family, there are a lot of people who left Europe for the United States, some of them in just the last century. I think it would be very sad if these close family links were to be overshadowed by a drift away.

# John Fund

## Columnist, *Wall Street Journal*

---

M Y THESIS IS THAT THE DIFFICULTIES we are seeing in European and American relations are in part a triumph of perception and style over substance and reality. At their core, things are not quite as bad as we perceive them to be, but issues of style and perception have governed the relations over the last few years.

There is definitely substance. The disagreement over the war in Iraq is real. The profound dislike of President Bush and his style and much of his Administration is certainly real, but certain issues of perception have compounded that. The complete breakdown of U.S. public diplomacy in the State Department and in various other entities of government has had a profoundly negative impact on the perception of the United States around the world.

I am not going to say whether incompetence has vied with incoherence in creating this situation. But let us be clear—the United States often does not know what its message is. It certainly cannot coherently explain it, and it certainly does not know how to tailor it to individual audiences.

A perfect example is the debate over the Niger uranium deposits, the forged documents and the intelligence reporting that Saddam Hussein had attempted to buy uranium from Niger. We now know that, believe it or not, substantially most of what the Bush administration claimed and what the government of Tony Blair claimed was true. We now know, believe it or not, that Ambassador Joseph Wilson was lying about almost everything that he said. We know this from documents from his wife and from him that were printed in the Senate Intelligence Committee's report last week. But it will not be reported. It will not be believed. In fact, it will be viewed as incredible. But it happens to be a fact.

Second, despite this complete breakdown in public diplomacy and despite this inability to communicate what is often a flawed American foreign policy—and I make no apologies for the many mistakes that led up to the war in Iraq and have continued since then—almost nothing that the United States could have done would have prevented the negative perceptions that were built up in Europe and elsewhere over the last couple of years, for two reasons.

First, the Bush administration is completely off, stylistically. There is almost nothing about it that appeals to European sensibilities. In fact, there is much about it that grates on them: the president's religiosity; the president's accent; the president's occasional inability to wrestle the English language to the ground and win; and the fact that he is from Texas. One of the leading presidents of a French think tank says, "He looks Texan. He smells Texan. We don't do Texas here." So the Bush administration stylistically was never going to be on good terms with the Europeans.

Second, there was a carefully planned, well thought-out and assiduously pursued campaign by former officials of the Clinton administration to denigrate this Administration, to talk down American foreign policy and to convince people that policy in the White House was being run by a buffoon. Now, I am not here to argue the relative intelligence of world leaders or their knowledge of world affairs. I will simply say this: in any situation and at any time when you tend to begin your discussions about another country and its leaders with the premise that they are stupid, that is a substitute for debate. It says more about the speaker's hubris than about the object's actual intelligence.

The Clinton-era officials did a very good job, because they had some ammunition. The Administration often made stumbles in foreign policy. The Clintonites assiduously cultivated the notion that these people were not to be trusted and certainly not to be supported.

This has extended to the point where it carries over to even the best ambassadors that America can send overseas—for example, Arnold Schwartzenegger, who grew up in Europe and who has many Austrian ties. He just represented the United States at the state funeral of the former Austrian president. Opinion polls in Austria show that while Arnold Schwartzenegger is respected and his success is admired, there is also a great deal of loathing and anger against him, because, as California's governor, he chose not to commute the sentence of a vicious convicted murderer who had been sentenced to the death penalty. Opposition to the death penalty is so profound in Europe and so universally held, at least among the elites, that it is almost impossible to have a clarifying argument about something that a California governor has no control over. He was simply carrying out the law as he is directed and is required to do, but he was nonetheless blamed for that. There is a great deal of opposition to him in Austria as a result of just that failure to act out certain social policies, regardless of the law.

The last two points I would make are about the European media resident in, and covering, the United States. It is fair to say that the mistakes the Bush administration stumbled into in Iraq were in part the result of "group think." When you get a bunch of likeminded people in a room constantly reinforcing each other, and all information is processed through a filter leading to the same conclusion, that is group think, and any outside messenger is excluded or ridiculed or discounted.

Group think has occurred many times over the years. The Bush administration suffered from group think and it is paying some of the price for that. However, there is another group think going on here—that of the European media that covers this Administration, because they all share the same view of it, of George W. Bush's intelligence, and about certain fundamental foreign policy and domestic issues, and they constantly reinforce each other.

Just as group think got the Bush administration into trouble, group think among the media entities that cover this country and this Administration, if it is completely one-sided in personal views, will seep into the coverage and it will have a limiting effect on describing reality accurately. It will tend to convey the country they want this nation to be, rather than the country it actually is.

My point about the parochialism of some of the European media is also relevant. I know how certain publications in this country tend to dominate the reading habits of Europeans. We at the *Wall Street Journal* are certainly next, but the *New York Times* and the *Washington Post* tend to dominate almost all of the reading matter that European correspondents take in. There is an awful lot more to read to understand this country, including UPI dispatches, *The National Interest*, and various other publications.

This country is not just the New York–Washington axis. People forget that now three states—California, Texas, and Florida—have 28 percent of the American population and about a third of its economic base. There is a lot going on in this country that does not take place in Washington or New York, and I tend to believe that Europeans view the rest of the country as a vast wasteland and the people in it not having any ideas of interest or note. That is a mistake.

My last point is that Israel is certainly a major subject of misunderstanding here. As a journalist, I am a generalist, but I also believe in some specialization. My form of specialization has been that in my entire journalism career, I have not written one single word on the Arab, Palestinian, and Israeli conflict. I am proud of that, because you can only get into trouble writing about it.

The conflict of visions that exists between how most people in the United States view the Arab-Israeli conflict, and how most people in Europe view the same conflict is irreconcilable. So long as the United States has an effective military and political alliance with Israel, there will be no possibility for understanding. As long as the Europeans tend to ignore the reality that the Palestinian Authority is made up of a bunch of thugs and thieves and liars, you are not going to have a full understanding of reality there either.

Where are we going? We are having an election coming up in November, and perception again will triumph over reality. The actual foreign policy differences between a John Kerry presidency and a Bush second term are not nearly as great as Europeans want them to be, wish them to be, hope them to be, or think they will be. American foreign policy under John Kerry or George Bush would about 85 percent overlap. However, the perceptions would be dramatically different. Europeans would embrace John Kerry, even more than they embraced Bill Clinton, because it would be such a refreshing break from the past and from the awful Texan.

But let us be clear, perception is not reality. The basic contours of American foreign policy would remain. We must not forget that John Kerry is an establishmentarian to his bones. He voted for the war in Iraq and he probably would still vote for the war in Iraq today, since enough pressure would be applied to him to do so and he bends to such pressure. American foreign policy is going to be fundamentally the same.

I will say we will have an easier time at cocktail parties if John Kerry is president, because stylistically he will be viewed as so superior. But the fundamental differences and misunderstandings between the U.S. and Europe will remain, and we are not going to conquer them until we square our perceptions of what we want the relationship to be with the actual reality.

# John O'Sullivan

## Editor, *The National Interest*

LET ME BEGIN WITH SLIGHTLY ENCOURAGING NEWS, because this has been a
cheerfully depressing occasion so far. The news is that people in American
journalism are aware that there is a problem with the coverage of international affairs.

After September 11th, the Pew International Journalism Program did an
opinion survey on the coverage of international news. It went to the editors of
218 newspapers with circulations of 30,000 readers and above and to people
who produce television news programs. Fifty-six percent of the editors
thought that their own publication's coverage of international news was either
fair or poor. Twelve percent said it was simply poor.

Two-thirds of respondents who looked at network news coverage on television thought it was poor, and 22 percent thought the networks did a poor job
as well. Cable television news did fairly better. Forty percent of the foreign editors described that as fair or poor. Overall, the ratings given to international
news coverage were significantly lower than those awarded to the media's coverage of sports, national news, local news, and business news.

Now, the editors in this survey did say that they thought things had improved slightly since September 11th, and—even more significantly—they
also said that reader interest in foreign and international coverage had increased since 9/11.

Why was there such relative lack of foreign news before? The first reason was
very obvious: the cost. Martin Walker's old newspaper had a very famous editor,
C. P. Scott, who was famous for the remark that "Comment is free, but facts are
sacred." That has been changed to "Comment is free, but facts are expensive." It

costs money to have a bureau in Beijing and Moscow and London. Very few papers that are not as large as *The Times* or magazines like *Time* and *Newsweek* can afford that kind of expenditure these days under conditions of enormous commercial competition, so they rely to a considerable extent—and very sensibly—on wire services.

But even there there is a problem. Being human beings, editors and reporters like to run work of their own, so there is always going to be a bias in the newsroom against outside contributions, and that translates into a bias against foreign and international coverage.

The second reason is that newspapers and television programs basically believe that the reader, the ordinary American, does not want coverage of international news. Instead, they want sports and business. They want national and, above all, they want local news.

Now, they are probably in part right about that. I say in part, because, in a sense, there is a reinforcing factor here. If your foreign news is not very good, then people will not watch it. And if they do not watch it, then you are not going to improve it.

Also, people have got to be convinced that much of the foreign news they get is going to have some kind of impact on their lives. Until September 11th, pictures of madmen in odd clothes running about shouting "Death to the Great Satan" were only of marginal interest. But now, they think that has a direct impact on their lives and are much more interested.

The good news here is that despite poor coverage, Americans by and large are not badly informed. Harris Interactive Polls puts out a number of surveys on American public opinion, and these show that although the public does not necessarily know the detail of international stories, they do have a pretty good grasp of the broad outline.

Asked to say which nations were close allies or friends of the United States and which were enemies, the respondents ranked twenty-five nations from friend to enemy pretty accurately. At the top of the scale, friends were Britain, Australia, Canada, and Israel and at the bottom, China, Colombia, and Pakistan. Obviously, Pakistan posed a bit of a problem for the people who had done the poll, since Pakistan was an ally of the United States. They reached the conclusion that television had shown a lot of anti-U.S. riots in Pakistan, and this had given the impression—not wholly false by any means—that the Pakistani people were anti-American even if their government was not.

In the same poll, which has been repeated over the course of twenty years, the views of ordinary Americans regarding their friends and enemies fluctuated more or less in line with international realities. Russia, for example, moved from being very definitely an enemy to being very definitely a friend. At the moment, it is about two-thirds down the list, and that reflects reality as well. Four years ago, China was seen as very hostile to the United States. By this year, it has become more friendly. Again, that is a reflection of real movement in U.S.-China relations—although Bill Gertz at the *Washington Times* might not agree.

France, very interestingly, has moved in the opposite direction. Fourteen percent of Americans used to regard France as an enemy. Now, fully 25 percent do. Obviously, that reflects a large number of things. For example, a few years ago a lot of publicity was given to the fact that there was a book out that reached the top of the bestseller list in France that claimed that September 11th was a fraud perpetrated by the U.S. government. That was not necessarily a long-term influence on U.S. attitudes. But for a while, it made people indignant.

Now, my own view of the French is that they can be tremendously annoying and troublesome right up to the moment when they actually come in on your side. They give you help, but they make you pay for it psychologically. Having said that, for most of the period since the Second World War, they have been fairly good allies of the United States. If that is changing now, and I think it is, it is fair to ask why.

On another topic, the U.S. role in the Arab-Israeli conflict, the judgments of the American people are as follows: in response to the question "Do you think that U.S. support is too one-sided?" Thirty-one percent believe it is too supportive of Israel, 6 percent think it is too supportive of the Palestinians, and 41 percent think the balance is about right. Twenty-one percent of those polled do not know, are not sure, or have not got a clue. So, broadly speaking, the Americans are getting that right. That, by the way, compares very favorably with the views of Arab and Muslim countries about the United States, which are extremely fanciful.

But there is another factor at play. There is a section of people who can get things completely out of kilter while being superficially well-informed on the details. I call this the "Noam Chomsky Effect," which means knowing everything about a topic except the essential facts. That is what you see with the controlled press in the Arab world, although with Al-Jazeera and others that may be beginning to change.

Now, when it comes to transatlantic relations, what has changed? Let me add a few points to those already mentioned.

One, obviously, is that the Cold War has ended. We do not have the absolute necessity to hang together in order to avoid being hanged separately that we used to have when the Soviet Union was still a threat. That has liberated certain negative tendencies in the relationship—tendencies which were always there. There have always been tensions, and on occasions like Suez they burst out into very bitter quarrels, but they were by and large held in check by the Cold War.

Second, there has always been a different political culture, broadly speaking, between Europe and the U.S., with the British and the other English-speaking countries stuck somewhere in the middle. On the Continent, this different political culture consisted of a greater willingness to support economic policies of state intervention and regulation and high levels of welfare paid by higher taxes. There was a greater preparedness to be deferential toward the United Nations and other international bodies. There were differences of social policy and attitude; elites have more power and the population is more deferential. So with the Cold War check removed, these different political attitudes are bound to produce an increasing number of clashes.

The third point is that there is a series of disputes within Europe itself regarding the future of Europe. To put it very simply, there are those who would like to create a European state that is also a power in the world, and there are those who, for various reasons, want something much looser, less regulated, less centralized, less national, less federal. We all know some of the lineup here. The British, obviously, would like to have a glorified free trade area; the French do as well, to a slightly lesser extent. The Germans would like a much more centralized state. And we know, too, that the balance of power may be changing with the arrival of the east and central Europeans into the EU. There are signs that in one or two cases, like Holland and Denmark, that there are strong political forces that have a hankering after the British view as well.

Now, in these circumstances, some European politicians actually have been prepared not only to embrace anti-Americanism in general, but to try to make America the basis for unifying Europe. They say: "Look, these people have too much power. If we are to have a check on their power, we ourselves have got to become more powerful, which means becoming more united." There is no doubt that anti-Americanism is being used as a building block by some in Europe, and it will inevitably go on being so used, even though any number of European politicians say that this has got to stop.

Finally, there is a difference of outlook, and a very important one, between the United States and Europe on international institutions, including the concept of the United Nations, its various agencies and the need for legitimacy that flows from them.

There is a real difference here. The United States is not only a superpower, it is a classical example of the post-Westphalian nation-state. It is a liberal, democratic nation-state. The EU, as it is developing, is claiming to be something else. Yes, it is getting a flag and an anthem, as well as an army of sorts. It is getting common citizenship. It is getting all of the things normally associated with nations or states..

In this case, however, the people who are most active in promoting European unity are denying this. They are claiming that it is a new, postnational kind of structure—one which cannot really be fully understood or realized as yet, but which fits in more comfortably than the United States does with the transnational structure of the EU, NGOs, and new forms of international law. The United States is wedded to the concept of national sovereignty and the EU has, in a sense, put national sovereignty behind it.

This is all nonsense, but it is seductive nonsense. There is a certain consistency about it, but it does mean that there will continually be a series of rows between Europe and America over the unwillingness of America to subject itself to the decisions of international bodies and so on. So Kyoto and the ICC are just the beginning of a long string of disputes.

And then we come to the final problem: American public diplomacy. You cannot expect the Europeans to listen to American objections to the ICC and Kyoto unless the Americans actually produce those objections. The U.S. State Department has simply failed, both in its relationship with the EU and its relationship with the UN, to lay out clearly a principled case as to why America finds it difficult to go along with things like the ICC.

That case is an important one. It has got a lot to do with where democratic legitimacy comes from. Is democratic legitimacy something states lend to international bodies, as I would argue, or is it something that exists "up there," as the EU would argue?

So far, the American positions on these things have been presented almost as arbitrary exercises of American power: "It doesn't suit us, we won't go along." In fact, there are good reasons for this American opposition, and those reasons would find in many Europeans a thoughtful audience. Not a sympathetic audience in all cases, but perhaps in some cases.

# Roland Flamini

## International Editor, United Press International

O NE OF THE PROBLEMS WITH SPEAKING LAST is that everybody has said almost everything that you intended to say, and the temptation is there to agree with all of them. The thing is, I am not entirely sure that I do.

The whole issue of media influencing transatlantic relations is an old story. It is a topic that has been around since immediately after the Second World War. Back then, Europeans were up in arms because the United States had decided that it needed a defense agreement with Franco's Spain. There was a great deal of rage expressed in the press from England all the way to, well, Germany. And then, of course, you have the opposition to Vietnam, which had a more scattered view of what was going on.

To a certain extent, Americans feel that they are well-informed about foreign affairs. But if a European visits the United States and looks for news about his country or the Continent in general, he would probably conclude that, in his absence, Europe has disappeared into a large black hole. For example, if you took yesterday's *Washington Post*, there was one story on Europe, and if you looked at the *Kansas City Star* for the last five days, there have been no European headline stories at all.

The information is coming from somewhere, but the information received is not enough to produce any substantial or intelligent reaction when a story does come along that needs to be covered—such as, for example, the debate over the French and European positions on the Iraq war. Instead, what you get is a rather simplified reaction of "Brits good, frogs bad," but nothing really substantial.

But it is not just the French. The Spaniards have suddenly become the whipping boys of the Bush administration and a large section of the press because of their decision to pull out of Iraq. So when Jose Maria Aznar lost the Spanish elections, the American press saw it as the Spanish electorate surrendering to terrorist pressure and turning to the Socialists.

Why? Because that has been the accepted view in Washington. In fact, of course, had they been reporting a little more and watching a little more closely, they would have known that every poll had forecast a close race, partly because more than two million young Spanish voters were coming into the electorate and nobody quite knew how they would vote—or whether they would vote at all. As it turned out, because of the bombing immediately before the election, they all did vote Socialist. But, in my opinion, that is largely because of how the Aznar administration actually handled the situation. The point is that one perhaps could have blunted some of the rhetoric and softened some of the rather aggressive language that was being used, even by the Administration.

The second point is that I agree to a certain extent that the press has been given a bum rap, particularly in this particular situation. The translated differences are not entirely the fault of the press. However, there is an anti-American bias which recurs in much of the European media. Again, not in all media, and not at the same time.

Last week, for example, European editors grabbed onto the question of whether the U.S. elections would or should be postponed in the event of a terrorist attack close to November 2nd. There was a great deal of interest in that, and the angle was: is this a Bush scare tactic? In other words, was it being brought up in order to make people vote for Bush, who as we all know in the polls is the man who is judged to be better able to handle the terrorist threat.

The third point is that today journalists are bombarded with reader and viewer reactions in real time, via email and voicemail. It happens to us here in the United States, but it happens even more in Europe. You finish a story and before you know it, you are getting all sorts of complaints from people. So the question is, who is influencing whom? Given the constant feedback, to what extent do editors make decisions based on what they believe the local audience is interested in? To what extent was coverage of Iraq shaped by whether the public was critical or whether it was supportive? European coverage of the Iraq war had a particular approach, which was entirely different from what we saw here in the United States.

Also, there is the enormous pressure of competition and ratings. In today's 24/7 news cycle, there is very little time for reflection. There is a treadmill quality to much in both the opinion and the reporting. The old fidelity to a particular newspaper or TV station that used to exist has been largely eroded; today, readers and viewers will cancel subscriptions at the drop of a hat.

European perceptions of the United States come with a lot of baggage. There are preconceived ideas which come from culture, from the movies, and even from personal perceptions of the U.S. The author Umberto Eco once told me that his first visit to the States was very irritating, because he realized that he previously had been writing about a fictitious country. This panic happens to a lot of Europeans when they finally confront the United States for the first time, which they are doing in increasing numbers—eleven million people crossed the Atlantic in both directions last year.

Finally, there is the ambivalence that some people have about what they really think about the U.S. In the film *Control Room*, which is a documentary about Al-Jazeera that I happen to think is actually better than *Fahrenheit 9/11*, the main interviewer at one point sits down and says that he has very negative views about America and does not like the Bush administration. He wonders how a country like the United States could actually like somebody like Bush. But he concludes by saying that, in fact, what he really wants for his children is to send them to the United States.

# IV

# Do Objective Differences in National Interests Dictate a Fundamental Shift in the U.S.-Europe Relationship?

# The Honorable Mark Lagon

United States Deputy Assistant Secretary
of State for International Organization Affairs

---

TRANSATLANTIC TENSIONS HAVE BEEN HIGH BEFORE: In 1956, when Washington opposed the Anglo-French invasion of Suez; in the late 1960s and early '70s, when thousands of Europeans took to the streets to protest the U.S. role in the Vietnam War; and in the early 1980s, when many Europeans protested Reagan administration plans to introduce intermediate-range nuclear missiles into Europe. Through times of tension, the partnership between the U.S. and Europe has remained, and the Atlantic partnership has been a central force for progress and prosperity in the world.

In the past year and a half, the durability of transatlantic relations has come to be questioned in a more profound way. The publics and media of America and Europe have focused more on what divides us than what unites us. What does divide us? And do the current tensions signal a fundamental shift in the relationship?

Historian and editorialist Robert Kagan observed, "Americans are from Mars and Europeans are from Venus. They agree on little and understand one another less and less." In actuality, the national interests of the United States and of our European allies are not so very different. Rather, the difference lies in our perceptions of the world based on our places in it and the methods we consequently choose to use in addressing threats.

Consider the national interests of Europe and the United States, which are—more often than not—shared interests. On counterterrorism, nonproliferation, trade issues, democracy, and human rights, the United States and Europe largely pursue the same goals. We both want to stem the proliferation of nuclear weapons, eradicate terrorism, see our populations prosper from our highly interconnected trade and investment with one another, usher in a new era of an expanding scope of global democracy, and protect what President Bush has called and the Europeans agree are the "non-negotiable demands of human dignity." Witness transatlantic cooperation on such key issues as combating terrorism, food aid, HIV/AIDS, and refugee assistance as proof that the United States and Europe can and often do work together with common purpose for the global good.

Where clashes occur, the problem lies not in interests but in perspective and methods. While the U.S. and Europe are often seen to be comparable political creatures, recent history has shown that perspectives on each side of the Atlantic are not always similar. Europe finds itself enjoying its longest run of peace thanks to the NATO alliance, as well as the success of a great experiment in history which has brought together on common ground the great, formerly-warring nations of Europe—facilitated for a half-century by an American security umbrella. The United States, on the other hand, views the world from its position as the world's greatest military power and faces associated global responsibilities.

Europe believes it has entered the early stages of a "perpetual peace" among democracies as Immanuel Kant envisaged, while the United States bears the responsibility of facing the complex and often-dangerous world outside the boundaries of that peace. Europe increasingly is focusing inward—on its own expansion, on integrating the economies of the former Warsaw Pact countries, and on its own social and economic challenges. After 9/11, America finds itself threatened from all sides, and with no choice but to look under every rock for threats so as to protect the lives and safety of its people.

For Europe, the "democratic peace" seems to have already arrived, requiring only multilateral negotiation and institutions to be maintained and expanded. Europeans assume those peaceful intentions, "rules" of dialogue and deals pertain to all international relations—such as in dealing with Iran—without giving due regard to the security framework that underpins it. For America, a democratic peace is an equally high priority—hence promotion of democracy as a central tenet of our statecraft—but it is only a hope, a far-from-completed dream for many other parts of the world. America sees no end to history, as Francis Fukuyama called it; not today. For us, the only sure path to global peace is indeed democracy, but that means that confronting dangerous undemocratic nations is a top priority and promoting democracy is essential. President Bush has declared that "lasting peace is gained as justice and democracy advance."

Our divergent perspectives lead America and Europe to choose different methods of confronting challenges. While multilateral diplomacy is an important tool of U.S. foreign policy, we are willing to engage in multilateralism only when it is effective and acknowledges consensus as a means to an end rather than an end in and of itself. In our view, it is a tragic mistake to value process over results. The desired result should not be consensus for its own sake or for the good of the organization, but relief for those who need it— food for the hungry, medicine for the sick, peace and reconciliation for the embattled, and political liberty for those who long for it.

For this reason, we value multilateral negotiations and agreements as a tool, but sometimes differ from our European allies in our view of how that tool should be used. For us, multilateralism is a key instrument of foreign policy, but not the only instrument, and not an end unto itself. We use multilateral processes if and when they are effective. If one multilateral instrument fails to work as intended or fails to live up to its founding principles, we are ready to turn to other multilateral instruments or to switch tactics entirely if necessary.

I will offer two brief examples before concluding. First, the Commission on Human Rights, where the emphasis on process over principle threatens to undermine the body's substantive work and its very credibility. Emphasis on consensus at the Commission on Human Rights has most recently produced unacceptable results with regard to the human rights crisis in the Sudan. President Bush has termed the brutalization of Darfur "a new chapter of tragedy in Sudan's troubled history," and has called on the government of Sudan not to remain complicit in it. As Secretary of State Colin Powell has said, "Need number one is security . . . so that the humanitarian effort can go on unimpeded." Clearly, the U.S. and Europe share the same interests and goals with regard to Sudan. Yet, despite agreement on the needs of the people of Darfur, this past April the European Union forewent its originally strong resolution on Sudan in order to pacify the African Union's demands for compromise. The U.S. sought to strengthen, and ultimately voted against, the resulting weak resolution at the Commission.

Rather than embrace compromise with the African group simply for the sake of consensus, we stood alone for what we believed in—the need for Sudan to respect the rights of its citizens. When Sudan was reelected to the Commission, the U.S. delegation walked out of the meeting and issued a public, very critical, statement. NGOs did not criticize us for unilateralism in this case.

Another issue on which Europe and the U.S. clearly share common interests is the threat of nuclear proliferation in Iran. Both the U.S. and Europe agree on the objective of stopping proliferation of nuclear weapons. We sometimes disagree on how to pursue that objective, particularly with regard to the multilateral framework of the International Atomic Energy Agency. Europe prefers to continue negotiations and discussion to resolve the dispute as long as they hold some prospects for success. However, the U.S. believes continued discussion only allows Iran to continue its long-standing practice of deception and delay, enabling it to clandestinely pursue sensitive nuclear technologies.

What is important is that the United States and Europe work together to press Iran to drop its dangerous nuclear fuel-cycle activities, and to ensure that the IAEA can and does carry out its responsibilities. The president has proposed, and we are discussing with our European friends and others, a number of initiatives to strengthen the effectiveness of the nuclear non-proliferation regime. These include an IAEA safeguards system and multilateral nuclear export control guidelines, initiatives designed to ensure that countries like Iran cannot pursue nuclear weapons under the guise of a peaceful nuclear program.

It is my view that, based on our common interests, the emerging shift in transatlantic relations is not grounds for, or signs of, a divorce. The United States and Europe have not come to see in the world different goals. Rather we have differing perspectives on the world, and hence sometimes choose different methods to reach those common goals. President Bush said recently, "Europe and America are linked by the ties of family, friendship and common struggle and common values. We're also bound to each other by common responsibilities." International peace, long-term stability, democracy building, economic development, humanitarian relief and human rights are in everyone's interest. Our approach to these interests should be guided, as President Bush has said, by "effective multilateralism . . . neither unilateralism nor international paralysis." The United States will be more successful if we do not have to pursue those goals alone, and we gladly look to the wisdom and cooperation of our friends "across the pond" to find effective multilateral solutions to global problems.

# The Honorable Dov Zakheim

## Former United States Undersecretary of Defense

A DDRESSING THE QUESTION OF WHETHER there is a fundamental difference between the United States and Europe begs two questions. The first is, what do you mean by Europe?

That is a serious question. As I see it, there are at least five different Europes right now. There is the core Europe, which might be the original European Economic Community: the Germans, Italians, Benelux, and French. Then there is what might be called the "outer core," the original European Free Trade Area Group: the British and the Scandinavians.

Then you have two, possibly even three other Europes. You have northeastern Europe, Poland (and the Czech Republic and Hungary), and the Baltic States. For the first time ever, because of their membership in NATO, these countries feel that they have turned the strategic corner, and are not simply living in the shadow of great powers with the kind of terror that divided them or consumed them every fifty or one hundred years or so. For these countries, there was a major, historical strategic shift, which they credit almost exclusively to the United States of America.

Southeastern Europe is different again. Countries that have clearly been liberated from the Soviet Union would like to see the United States even more engaged. It is not enough simply to get into NATO; they want bases. There is a hankering amongst these countries for even more evidence of American commitment, something that I think the Baltic States, the Poles, and Hungarians already assume is there.

Then you have other countries, such as Ukraine, which don't fit into any of the four previous categories. So to talk about Europe in an undifferentiated way is a mistake.

Now, let us get to the second question: are there fundamental differences? What do we mean by this? There can be no doubt there are differences, but are these fundamental? The answer is, probably not.

Look at Afghanistan. If you go to the headquarters of the International Security Force (ISAF) there, you will meet colonels from a lot of countries, overwhelmingly European, who clearly share the American sense that there was a fundamental threat to the West from a country that harbored terrorists, destabilized its neighbors, and had returned its own people to the sixteenth century, at best. We were not unilateral on this. The French looked at the issue exactly the way we did. The Germans are there. So are the Swedes. We have created what are called provincial reconstruction teams, and the Scandinavians are taking over one of those. Clearly, there is a sense of common value.

Let us turn to Iraq. I found it fascinating that the Hungarians came to tell me that even when things really turn sour in Iraq, they will not leave. Ukrainians are not leaving. The Spanish were there, after all—although the election showed that most Spaniards did not like that. Most of the countries are not pulling out. To talk about "Europe" in this context is basically to fall into the French trap, because France wants us to think, wants everybody to think, that France is Europe and Europe is France. But even France itself is of two minds on this—otherwise, they would not be with us in Afghanistan.

The third case, and maybe the most controversial of all, is Israel/Palestine. Many people tend to forget, but President Bush not only has stated publicly that he stands squarely behind Israel's security, he is also the first president who has actually said that he is prepared to accept a Palestinian state. Now, if indeed you get a unity government in Israel, which includes the Labor component led by somebody like Shimon Peres, the gap between Europe and the United States immediately begins to close, for the simple reason that you are likely to have a deputy prime minister who is committed to a very different policy than the prime minister. Peres will not join that government unless Israel is prepared to bend a little bit on what it is prepared to do with the Palestinians. To the extent that the Israelis bend, the gap between the Americans and the Europeans begins to narrow.

I have always considered myself a realist Republican. So I would say that leaving aside people from Mars, people from Venus, Wilsonians and so on, the fundamental differences between us simply are not there. What unites the United States and Europe may have changed somewhat. But now that there are new European players, whatever bonds have dissipated with respect to some of our older allies have been more than compensated for by some of our newer ones. When NATO voted on Iraq, for example, it was 16 to 3 in favor of the United States' position. That suggests that, although it is probably counterintuitive, we are closer to Europe than we have been in the past.

# Yossef Bodansky

## Director of Research, International Strategic Studies Association

L ET ME LOOK AT EMERGING THREATS, and the impact that may have on U.S.-European relations. They include international terrorism, the issue of state sponsorship of terrorism, narcoterrorism, and the proliferation of weapons of mass destruction and ballistic missiles—an area where Europe is still a major source of technology and the number one site of money laundering. All of these things feed the collapse and radicalization of third world states.

Essentially, there are two issues that divide us. One is more philosophical; Europe has a penchant for negotiation with the barbarians at the gate, while the United States has a penchant for proactive prevention of threats before they hit us.

But I am far more interested in what I call the practicalities and the technicalities of doing business with these issues. And there, I am in full agreement that the further consolidation of an EU that takes over issues like Interpol, the continent-wide intelligence service, and so on is going to have a detrimental effect, not only on the national security of EU member states, but on that of the United States as well. Because the key to addressing all of the issues I have outlined here is intelligence and special operations and clandestine activities—the crown jewels of each and every state.

The United States has had excellent relations with some governments in Europe. We have had profound cooperation on the most intimate of issues. But we also have a profound mistrust of other European governments. Even though there is plenty of tourism to and from these countries, and we import their wine or their cheeses, we still mistrust them thoroughly.

As the EU continues to consolidate and bring together its law enforcement, intelligence, military, and other elements outside the framework of NATO and other institutions that the U.S. can supervise, the natural tendency is to look to bring cooperation down to the lowest common denominator. Therefore, countries that would otherwise have been beneficiaries of closer cooperation with us no longer are, and we—who benefited tremendously at one time from very close cooperation—no longer do so either.

There are three issues that worry me most. From my dealing with European colleagues over the last few years, I see profound gaps emerging in attitudes toward crises that will have a dire impact on the entire world.

First, the internationalization of domestic terrorism in Europe. Local networks are now becoming the most common and solid foundation of Islamist operations in Europe. Nor do these extremists operate only in Europe itself. For example, the suicide bomber whose attack brought down the United Nations building in Baghdad was a product of a European network who was sent to Iraq because he would not be detected by American or other intelligence services. It is imperative for us to know more about these networks because of Iraq, and because they are using places like Hamburg to build capabilities through which to strike at the United States.

With regard to the European police, security forces, and intelligence services, two things are happening. First, the Europeans know far, far less than they did in the past, and they do even less about it. And second, we have a major problem with cooperating with them.

Another issue is a question of outreach and preemption against major emerging crises—not just a spectacular terrorist strike that is being planned, but major international crises that will have direct impact on European economy and stability, and on ours. For example, what are we going to do about the collapse of Saudi Arabia? Are we going to wait for Saudi Arabia to go up in flames before we go and clean up the mess? We need the oil. The Western economy cannot survive without Saudi oil and the oil reserves of Saudi Arabia, so we will have to intervene. But do we wait as the Europeans urge us to, or do we have to do something more preemptive?

What are we going to do about the succession crisis in Egypt? Do we have to wait for the closure of the Suez Canal before we wake up?

What are we going to do about Morocco? The king there was the protégé of the French. What is going to happen to the Strait of Gibraltar if Morocco becomes radically Islamic?

Europe will not, as an institution, talk about the criteria for preventive intervention. Can we in the United States afford to wait and see if these things happen? On the other hand, when it was imperative to take a unilateral step—even imperfectly, as we have done—the Europeans began screaming and . . . well, we all know the rest of the story.

Last, but not least, is the issue of foreign economic interest. Here, there is an emerging clash on two fronts. One is technology transfers and money laundering in Europe itself. Europeans or EU institutions, in the name of privacy, are loathe to undertake any strong measures in order to contain such activities. And we will pay the price, because at the end of the day we are the "Great Satan" and most of these acquisitions are done in order to confront us.

The other issue is how to deal with emerging rogue states in the third world, where there are a lot of rare metals and other strategic resources that are crucial to the high-tech economy that makes the information age possible? The Europeans urge negotiation, compromising with local strong-men and, essentially, becoming a hostage to their whims. We, on the other hand, have been thinking about sterner measures, like helping the democratic movements in those countries.

At the end of the day, there will be conflict, because these two approaches are incompatible. Moreover, these crises are not happening because of politics or politicians in the United States or Brussels or anywhere else in Europe. They are happening because of developments in the Muslim world, in the developing world.

We will need to address these issues. So will the Europeans, because they are dependent on these economic resources as much as we are. Unless we want to compromise our ability to deal with such challenges, we had better find a way to somehow bridge the gap between us and "the other side of the pond." However, having dealt with those countries on these practical matters, I am very pessimistic that we can do so.

# Carl Gershman

## President, National Endowment for Democracy

I HAVE BEEN ASKED TO COMMENT on whether the objective differences between the United States and Europe dictate a fundamental shift in their relationship. There are five such differences, each of which pulls in the direction of greater transatlantic division.

The first involves different concepts of sovereignty. The United States adheres to a concept of state sovereignty that goes back to the Treaty of Westphalia of 1648. Although the U.S. is a party to countless multilateral treaties and is integrated into the global economy, we continue to think of ourselves as a sovereign nation-state governed by leaders who are accountable to a national electorate and pledged to defend U.S. national security. By contrast, in Europe the principle of state sovereignty is giving way to a process of integration into the European Union. At present, this process is absorbing much of Europe's energies, with the result that European countries are increasingly inward-looking and concerned with internal and regional issues, while the U.S. remains a global power with worldwide strategic and security interests. Moreover, at a time when the war on terrorism has strengthened U.S. resolve to defend these interests, with military force if necessary, the integration process in Europe has fostered the emergence of a postnational mind-set that is averse to conflict and the use of force and looks almost exclusively to multilateral negotiation as the path to peace and stability.

This leads to the second objective difference, which is a vast and growing discrepancy in military capability. Not only does the U.S. spend three times as much as all of the members of the EU combined on military defense, but it has a unified force structure, whereas Europe's forces and command structure

are divided among twenty-five countries. This compounds the military im-
balance and reinforces the European aversion to the use or projection of military force as an instrument of foreign policy.

The third difference is economic. Relative to Europe, the U.S. economy is
dynamic and risk-oriented and its labor market is flexible. State control is far
more pronounced in Europe, especially in France, Germany, and Italy. The
labor markets are much more regulated than in the U.S. (*The Economist* calls
them "sclerotic"), leading to lower rates of growth. There is pressure in Europe
to change this—for example, there is growing opposition to the thirty-five-
hour week, which was meant to increase the number of jobs but has had the
opposite effect by lowering productivity. But for now, key European countries
are less competitive economically than the U.S.

The fourth difference is demographic. In Europe, the number of births per
woman is 1.5, which is lower than the number needed to maintain the exist-
ing population, whereas in the U.S. it is 2.0. European populations are declining, whereas the U.S. population is slated to increase by 26 percent during the
first quarter of this century. In addition, the Muslim minority in France, Germany, and other European countries is a steadily growing part of the population. The long-term strategic implications of these trends are enormous.

Finally, I would argue that the U.S. is a country that is trying to change the
world, if not in its own image than at least in the direction of greater human
freedom, whereas Europe is more oriented to maintaining the status quo. This
is not new, but it does lead to different approaches to dealing with the problem of autocratic systems in the Middle East, for example.

That said, it is important to emphasize that there are countervailing points
that the U.S. and Europe have in common. The most important is that, for all
their differences, the U.S. and Europe share democratic values in common. We
may have somewhat different priorities, with Europe putting much more
stock in multilateral institutions such as the International Criminal Court.
But there is no significant group of countries anywhere in the world with
which the United States has more in common in terms of a commitment to
the values of democratic civilization.

We also share in common fundamental security interests. We are united in a
shared commitment to the nonproliferation of nuclear weapons and especially
to the elimination of terrorism as a threat to our common security. The threat
of terrorism is driving the U.S. and Europe to seek new forms of cooperation,
not just in intelligence-sharing but increasingly in the development of common
strategies to assist the countries of the broader Middle East to develop competitive market economies and stable, inclusive democratic institutions.

The recent accession of new Central European democracies into NATO and
the EU will only strengthen transatlantic cooperation. Given their geographic

proximity to Western Europe and their political and philosophical affinity with American democracy, the countries of Central Europe are poised to play an important bridging function in strengthening transatlantic cooperation.

For this to happen, though, the U.S. will have to act more decisively on the common interests it has with Europe. In any relationship, one is always free to emphasize the positive or the negative. In dealing with Europe, the U.S. should start from the understanding that we are both members of the same community of values. We need to look for opportunities to build this partnership by developing new forms of cooperation that address both the threats and the challenges that we must face together in the twenty-first century. These threats can divide us, but they can also be seen as an opportunity to rebuild the transatlantic relationship on a new foundation.

By seizing this opportunity, we can end the transatlantic drift and begin to fashion a common strategy for democracy and security.

www.ingramcontent.com/pod-product-compliance
Lightning Source LLC
Chambersburg PA
CBHW021823270326
41932CB00007B/307